Love and Limerence:

Harness the Limbicbrain

Love and Limerence:
Harness the Limbicbrain

Lynn Willmott & Evie Bentley

Lathbury House Limited

Copyright Lathbury House Limited 2012

First Published 2012
Second Edition 2013, USA 2014

Copy edited Sally Neal, Dallas, Texas.

The rights of Lynn Willmott and Evie Bentley to be identified as the authors of this work has been asserted in accordance with the Copyright Designs Act 1988.

All rights reserved. Except for the quotation of short passages for the purpose of review: no part of this publication may be reproduced, stored in a retrieval system, or transmitted in any form, or by any means electronic, mechanical, photocopying, recording or otherwise, without the prior permission of the authors.

With kind permissions: John Bradshaw Media Group; LOVE SICK by Frank Tallis, Published by Arrow. Reprinted by permission of The Random House Group Ltd; Penguin Random House, USA; Keep It Simple Books, USA.; Hay House Inc., New York.; The Guilford Press, New York; Scarborough House, Lanham, Maryland; USA, GRAMPS.

ISBN – 978-1481215312
ISBN – 148 1215310

Acknowledgements

We would like to thank the clients and friends, whom in sharing their diverse limerence stories, informed us and now an even wider audience - their insight was essential. We are especially grateful to those who asked for their words to be shared in order to promote awareness of Limerence. Thank you to the online communities. Thank you to the reviewers (literal and cyber) for their insight and useful suggestions. Thanks also to Dr Sue Churchill and Dr Alison Taylor with whom the limerence concept was first discussed. Thanks to Mandi Lines Personal Trainer, Jennifer Hargreaves Nutrition Therapy Practitioner, Paul Willmott for the photography. Thanks also to Tim Croft for cover design and Ed Fox design technician. Lastly thanks to Malcolm and Kate McIlhagga, at Zenlo, for web design and enthusiasm.

L. W.

Thank you to my parents for loving and looking after us all. Thank you to special friends S.G., S.P., L.B. and P.S.

E. B.

I want to thank the friendship network whose everyday help and support are always wonderful: thank you alumnae, swimming friends, Sussex friends and of course the punk rock gig-goers – you are amazing.

We dedicate this book to those Limerent Experiencers who may stIll be enveloped, as well as to those whom have already journeyed through. Know that you were never alone, that recovery is always an option and that the future is yours to craft.

Contents

Abbreviations

Preface

Introduction	**1**
Definitions & Background Theory	1
Therapeutic Case Study One	16
Therapeutic Case Study Two	20
Chapter 1. Foundation & Coexisting Conditions	**23**
Biological Basis	23
Attachment	27
Limerent Demographics	33
Age	34
Gender	34
Triggers	37
Relationship of Limerence to Other Traits	41
Interactional Effects	45
Chapter 2. Individual & Social Effects of Limerence	**49**
Rejection	49
Starvation	56
Minimal Attention	59
Full Reciprocation or Consumption	62
Transference	63
Friendship	64
Chapter 3. Practical Strategies Part 1: Replacing Addictive Ruminative Thinking with Rational Thinking.	**67**
Signs	67
Real LO	71
Imagined LO	73
Chapter 4. Practical Strategies Part 2: Interrupting Addictive & Compulsive Behaviour	**81**
Boundary Issues	81
No Contact	89
Limited Contact	93
Eye Contact	95
Disclosing to LO	97
Disclosing to SO or Spouse	103
Disclosing to Friend or Colleagues	104

Contents Cont.

Chapter 5. Practical Strategies Part 3: Insight & Therapeutic Intervention	**109**
Self as Saviour	109
Therapeutic Writing	116
Virtual Support Networks	118
Psychological Therapy	119
Pharmaceutical Therapy	124
Avoiding Reescalation & Reoccurrence	125
Chapter 6. Practical Strategies Part 4: Inspirational Aspects of Limerence	**131**
Food	131
Exercise	132
Physical Appearance	134
Artistic Expression	135
Acquisition of Knowledge & Skills	136
Meditation	137
Philosophies	139
Conclusion	**147**
References	**151**
Biography	**167**
Recommended Reading List	**169**
Virtual Support Resources	**171**
Research	**173**
Authors	**175**

Abbreviations:

Abbreviations used represent those that Limerent Experiencers commonly use themselves. For this book's purposes, LO, LE or SO regards both the singular and plural.

LE	=	Limerent Experiencer (s)
LO	=	Limerent Object (s)
SO	=	Significant Other (s)
NC	=	No Contact
LC	=	Limited Contact

Preface

All sorts of different people become a Limerent Experiencer (LE), having involuntarily attached to an object of adoration—their Limerent Object (LO)—and are baffled by their apparent lack of control and entrapment to the condition while an episode plays out. In limerence, there is often an overwhelming need to attempt to *create and make sense of the story* about *what happened,* however, unlike other life scenarios, many hold back from telling anyone. This is particularly unfortunate given that when sudden, unexpected and overwhelming experiences occur in our lives (which they are sometimes apt to do), it can be both useful and healing to consider, then share some of the details with other people with whom there is a relationship of trust.

Often LE may not be familiar with the concept or term limerence, since it seems that frequently it is stumbled across while searching the internet about related behaviours such as obsessive love or love addiction. For some LE, the negative feelings associated with the state may have prevented them from seeking help or there may be physical barriers involved, such as having a Significant Other (SO) or spouse, with some deeming their choice of LO inappropriate, such as in the case of close family friends or other peoples' SO or spouse etc. Such that in many cases, the LE inclination toward identifying and locating a suitable confidante with which to seek support regarding their limerent experience may be hampered as a potentially risky and complicated decision.

When LE do tell someone about their *story,* it seems some use discussion forums, which could be particularly beneficial since such services have the ability to include informational, emotional, and companionship support, as well as confidentiality. Additionally, some LE ultimately identify and locate professional support. However, it is noted that at present, the condition is without diagnosis criteria or treatment plan and there are few recognised and organised informational resources available and as such, the types and quality of professional support may be diverse. Some LE simply use forms of self-help, whereby they read associated books or search the internet for information that seems relevant to their limerent experience.

So it seems that by whatever process LE sought to *create and make sense of their story,* and whether and how they choose to obtain support, can differ in accordance with individual attributes as well as personal circumstances. Ultimately, whether an external source of support is used or whether the journey in the limerent experience occurs in private, it appears that it is the attempts to *regain personal control and disentrapment to the condition* and the need to *create and make sense of their story* that become paramount for moving on psychologically and literally toward a *better place*.

Dorothy Tennov recognised in her original book in 1979 (*Love and Limerence: The Experience of Being in Love*) that there was a need to create *stories* coupled with a reluctance to share them. Her book was aimed at "taming a madness (here called limerence) by learning its habits, identifying it various parts and forms, and hoping thereby to make some predictions about its course" (p173). Thus, this book *Love and Limerence: Harness the Limbicbrain* also aims to be a collection of ideas and themes with which to aid LE in creating and making sense of their own limerent *story*, through considering the common feelings, thinking, behaviours and experiences of other LE. However, in extension to Tennov (1999; 2005), the aim of this book is also to include many suggestions on how to cope with the limerent experience and how to achieve satisfactory resolution of unpleasant attributes associated with the state. For some LE, their personal aim may be to regain personal control and dis-entrapment of the condition and/or to regain working memory capacity, rational noncompulsive thinking, self-esteem, self-dignity, sanity, as well as being able to better engage in normal behaviour, pass exams, keep their job, their significant relationship or marriage etc. However many and diverse the particular motivations may be, the main consideration within this book is that there is some recognition from the LE that a change is necessary or prudent in terms of their current feelings, thinking, behaviour, and experiences regarding the limerent episode or, generally, their lives.

However, a caveat then—we recognise that not all will see limerence as a wholly negative state, indeed many would not have wanted to have missed the highs to save from experiencing the lows, as someone would have surely said. Indeed, if you are happily limerent (congratulations and long may it last), you may enjoy this book as a point of reference for later on (hopefully, you will never need it). Moreover, we concur that often LE have come to regard a limerent episode as an albeit painful but positive life-changing experience in which they were inspired to stop old negative habits and activities in favour of a generally more healthier lifestyle, resulting in becoming physically fitter and more invested in their physical appearance. Some LE describe how the experience resulted in acquiring new skills and knowledge, with some even considering the experience as an emotional, intellectual, or spiritual awakening. Thus the intention for this book is that it could be used for promoting awareness, as a coping manual regarding the less pleasant aspects of the limerent experience and as a tool toward recognizing the many potential benefits that may be afforded. The book is both a guide for people who believe themselves to be limerent and are trying to recover, in whatever sense that might be, as well as a resource for those interested in the subject, including therapists and academics.

The information contained in the book is by no means exhaustive of the limerent experience, nor is it our intention to be authoritative, but rather there is an attempt to cover the main opinions that LE describe, with these *themes* denoted in italics. These opinions relate to peer review journal articles, general release sources (literal and cyber), therapeutic cases, friends (literal and cyber) and own experiences. Thus the evidence presented is diverse with balanced contribution throughout. However, note that no formal systematic thematic analysis has been performed. As such, these opinions are pertinent to a select group and the extent to which they represent substantive numbers of LE has not been assessed. Furthermore, since at present very few published sources specifically regard the topic of limerence, references may be cited that appear to relate to limerence, with straight brackets [ ] sometimes used to show where the limerent reference has been inserted for clarity purposes. In the therapeutic cases and comments, all details are fictionalised. Where a contributor has given express permission for their words to appear either unchanged or with minor modification, we believe the source of their communication, be it in any medium, to be untraceable at the time of publication. Notwithstanding the above, any similarity to any persons, living or dead, is entirely coincidental.

The *Introduction* outlines the definitions and background theory of limerence from an academic perspective. Chapter One, *Foundations and Co-existing Conditions,* considers limerence from its biological basis and attachment issues, giving explanation to the biological role of the limbic system, which gave rise to the metaphor *harness the limbicbrain!* The demographics of limerence experiencers and common triggers for their limerent episodes are reviewed, as is the relationship of limerence to other states and traits. Chapter Two, *Individual and Social Effects of Limerence,* regards in particular the role of rejection, starvation, minimal attention, full reciprocation or consummation, transference and friendships as potential episode events, and outcomes. Chapter Three, *Practical Strategies Part 1: Replacing Addictive Ruminative Thinking with Rational Thinking,* describes the use of signs in the limerent experience and the need to differentiate between the real vs the imagined LO. Chapter Four, *Practical Strategies Part 2: Interrupting Addictive & Compulsive Behaviour,* covers issues such as the need to respect boundaries, the use of No Contact or Limited Contact and Eye Contact in terms of recovery, also the important decision regarding whether to disclose limerent thoughts and feeling and to whom to disclose. Chapter Five, *Practical Strategies Part 3: Insight & Therapeutic Intervention,* regards the Self as Savior, including the use of therapeutic writing, virtual support networks, psychological or pharmacological therapies, as well as the need to avoid reescalation and reoccurrence of unwanted limerence attributes. Chapter Six, *Inspirational Aspects of Limerence,* reports on potential positive effects regarding food, physical appearance, exercise, artistic expression, acquisition of knowledge and skills, meditation, and philosophies.

Just as in Tennov's original work, we have focused on the individual experience of the LE, rather than the experience of the LO per se. Indeed, in our view, Baumeister & Wotman (1992) have already provided an excellent juxtaposition of both sides of unrequited love, being one of the common trends in limerence. We would happily review the topic of limerence from the point of view of being a LO, but feel that it is the LE whose stories need to be considered first. Like Tennov, we are also aware of the potential social discomfort in regard to reviewing topics of love variances, but have felt that such was the need for an extension of her work to provide a contemporary overview and a coping resource, that only these latter considerations should be paramount. We genuinely believe LE may be interested in this book, and it is to them firstly and foremost that the book is dedicated. Given the authors backgrounds, the book has been written in academic style as a comprehensive review of the subject. Lastly, in the interest of simplicity, we have not distinguished between which author is speaking at any one time, to this extent our contribution to the book is truly shared.

Note to the LE: Immediate practical strategies for coping can be found in chapters Three, Four, Five, and Six.

Limerence is all about YOU, and only YOU can make the positive changes in your life, such that the limerent experience becomes the inspirational gift that it can be – giving insight, empowerment and enlightenment.

Love and Limerence:

Harness the Limbicbrain

Introduction

Limerence was originally described by psychologist Dorothy Tennov in her 1979 book *Love and Limerence: The Experience of Being in Love,* which reviewed stories, interview and questionnaire data describing limerent experiences. The topic was revisited in a 2005 e-book, *A Scientist Looks at Love and Calls it Limerence: The Collected Works of Dorothy Tennov.* For Tennov (2005), key features of limerence included "excessive thinking about the Limerent Object, irrationally positive evaluation of their attributes, emotional dependency, and longing for reciprocation" (p17). More recently, Wakin & Vo (2008) defined limerence as "an involuntary interpersonal state that involves intrusive, obsessive, and compulsive thoughts, feelings, and behaviours that are contingent on perceived emotional reciprocation from the object of interest" (p1). Contrary to Tennov, Wakin & Vo (2008) emphasis the negative attributes of the state, suggesting it is "necessarily negative, problematic, and impairing, with clinical implications" (p1).

Limerence may be aligned to infatuation, lovesickness, romantic love, love addiction, obsessive love, or affection deficit disorder, as well as faux love and in love with being in love. Indeed, the original author, Tennov (1999), notes "To be in the state of limerence is to feel what is usually termed "being in love" (p16). However, Tennov sought to use the term limerence, so as not to show disrespect for the state of love or to offend those who had not experienced limerence (as if they were bereft of love). While the early stages of limerence may share similarities with other forms of love (e.g. both limerence and new love often involve persistent and distracting thoughts for each other), thereafter the intensity of feeling induced in limerence can quickly become uncomfortable to the Limerent Experiencer (LE) and to the object of their adoration and attachment, the Limerent Object (LO).

Typically, securing reciprocation from the chosen LO becomes paramount over all other considerations, such that the LE has in fact detoured from love. The process of limerence soon comes to play little real regard or care for the well-being of the LO, impacting negatively on the prospect of a healthy romantic bonding where there may be shared interests and enjoyment of each other's company. Ultimately, what best defines the state of limerence is perhaps that "it defies control" (Tennov, 1999. p256) and that it can "[re-order] the motivational hierarchy, with consequent disruption or neglect of other interests, relationships, and responsibilities" (Tennov, 2005. p10). As such Wakin & Vo (2008) add in that, in limerence, any initial feelings and reactions associated with love become more "intense, pervasive and disruptive"(p2).

Tennov (1999) suggested that limerence was "a certain state that some people were in much of the time, others in some of the time, but still others never in, or at least not yet" (p15). For those in a more or less permanent state of limerence, she described how the beginning and end of each episode could involve a state of "readiness" (p106). With any limerent experience occurring spontaneously, in the form of a love at first sight, or more slowly. However, even in the latter case the LE can often cite a specific point in time that their feelings became limerent. She notes that importantly the limerence desire regards emotional reciprocation, it is more than just sexual attraction or initial inclination toward sex. Tennov (1999) ascribed the following signs to the limerent experience:

1. Intrusive thinking of LO (a possible sexual partner)
2. Longing for reciprocation
3. Interpretation of LO actions toward reciprocation alters LE's mood
4. Limerent to one person (unless early or fading limerence)
5. Imagination of LO reciprocation can bring temporary relief
6. Shyness and fear of rejection
7. Adversity can intensify limerence
8. Attendance to *signs* of hidden passion (realistic or not)
9. Heartache especially in uncertainty
10. A feeling of walking on air in perceived reciprocation
11. Other concerns go to the background
12. Regarding LO as admirable and not dwelling on the negative, with compassionate perception able to render the latter to a positive attribute.

Tennov (1999) described how, once the LO is identified, a process of *crystallization* takes place (as per the theory of Stendhal, 1822), whereby the attractive attributes of the LO are emphasised and less attractive attributes largely ignored. Tennov (1999) notes that recent accounts regard the alternative term *idealisation*, which gives greater emphasis to the less attractive attributes being ignored, such that "the image is molded to fit a preformed, externally derived, or emotionally needed conception" (p31). Whereas, for Tennov, in limerence, less attractive attributes are "usually seen, but emotionally ignored" (p31), along with the overemphasis of attractive attributes with even neutral attributes turned positive. She goes on to note that the course of limerence usually involves a pleasurable rapid rise in intrusive thinking about the LO's positive attributes, until *first crystallization* (as per Stendhal, 1822), representing approximately 30% of a waking day thoughts. Then under the continued conditions of hope and uncertainty, by the *second crystallization,* the limerence strength can represent as much as near 100%, approximately, of a waking day's thoughts. At this time, limerence can be "ecstasy, or it may be despair" (p44), and thereafter, the pattern may rise or fall. The following summarises the course of the limerent experience:

1. The limerent reaction occurs at a specific recallable point. The LO is a possible sexual partner; with some, there is a physical attraction, although not necessarily a sexual attraction.
2. Thinking about the LO becomes pleasurable, with a feeling of freeness, and perceived responses are considered to regard LO's

positive attributes. At this stage, it is possible to have more than one potential LO.
3. Potential reciprocation from the LO can be euphoric, there is a persistent review of LO's positive attributes, replaying interactions and increased consideration to one's own relevant attributes.
4. Limerence increases where obstacles exist or where there are doubts about LO reciprocation. Eventually, even the possibility of undesirable attributes of the LO will not cause the limerent experience to desist (crystallisation). Attempts are made to improve physical appearance and/or any status in order to increase desirability, and there is an increasing fear of rejection.
5. With doubt and hope regarding reciprocation rumination can reach 100% being euphoric or despair. Rumination may be interrupted by, activities such as those that might better endure the LE to the LO (e.g. beautification) or impress the LO, alternatively and preferably actual interaction with the LO. This status remains while hope and uncertainty exist.
6. Where reciprocation is received limerence stabilises until the next period of uncertainty. Intensity can increase since signs of interest may be perceived to be concealed.

Tennov (1999) described the role of physiological states of excitement and fear in association with the limerent experience and how they are often, unfortunately, detrimental to the overall aim, which is emotional reciprocation. She also described LE attempts to hide signs of interest and over-ascribe and analyse any possible signs from the LO, thus leading to a kind of "paranoia" (p72). She reports how *fear of rejection* becomes increasingly significant as the episode plays out, causing pain while also enhancing desire. Additionally, she notes the frequent role of external obstacles in the limerent experience, such as parental objection or marriage. Lastly, it is noted how the limerent experience can have wide spreading effects, such as when sexual interest is heightened, but directed to someone other than the LO, such as the LE significant other (SO) or spouse, though more often this is not the case.

Three key relationship types were described—affectionate bonding, mutual limerence and more commonly unreciprocated limerence, whereby one is limerent the other not (note: she sought to distinguish this type of unrequited experience from those where no commitment to a relationship existed). In terms of affectionate bonding relationships, being the more common cultural representation of love as regarding concern and care, many have not contained limerence, or it may have been mutual at the start, more likely one partner was limerent (often with concealment attempts) and the other was not. She also noted four further possibilities being:

1. Sexually active, limerent
2. Not sexually active, but limerent
3. Sexually active, but not limerent
4. Not sexually active, not limerent

This is presented with the presumption that the scenario whereby both partners are sexually active and limerent would be the most blissful, though also the least likely to endure.

Tennov (1999) suggests there are going to be many people who have never experienced limerence (or not yet) and there are likely also to be some people who have experienced limerence, but only as the LO. Indeed, she reports how non-limerent partners often describe the unpleasantness of their status as LO, including feeling suffocation, and how they are aware that they often unintentionally hurt their limerent partners feelings (Tennov, 1999; 2005). Interestingly, however, she notes how often it is the LE that breaks such relationships. But where the LE does not break off the relationship and the LO makes the rejection, Tennov (1999) notes the likely process of grief for the unfortunate LE, including aspects of shock and depression and even incidences of self-injury or suicide, along with damage to property or others. She proposes that what may in part separate more private from proactive reactions from individual LE, along with their ability to have learned from any earlier episodes and their perceptions about the LO actions, often regards whether there was any evidence of hope for potential reciprocation. In such cases, she notes the role that rage might play, together with anger and jealousy.

Tennov (1999; 2005) notes that, once limerence begins, the trajectory will be determined by the LO's behaviour and its interpretation by the LE. With unsuitability not regarded (e.g. religion, marriage etc.), rather such factors may become "obstacles" with which the episode can thrive, albeit that unsuitability may impact on how the limerent episode is played out publicly (Tennov, 1999. p182). Limerent episodes on average have a minimum duration of 1-3 years to 7 years, with few dissipating within 6 months and some lasting decades. Where limerent relationships do persist, it may be because another kind of bonding supplants it or circumstances have hampered disengagement, but she highlights the danger that the previous limerent partner may then become limerent for someone else, "hence a series of marriages and divorces" (Tennov, 1999. p143). She cites outcomes for the cessation of limerence being: consummation, starvation, or transformation. In consummation (meaning full reciprocation), there may become a more lasting love or a less positive state, whereas in starvation, signs of hope are dashed against evidence to the contrary from the LO. Lastly, transformation involves limerence being recalibrated to a new LO (given that limerence in full flood regards only one object at a time). Later, Tennov (2005) used somewhat different descriptions of the possible 'escape routes' as being "reciprocation or removal of all possibility thereof and transference" (p354). Tennov (2005) created an algorithm or law of limerence as follows:

1. Person A may be in a state of receptivity to limerence, the Person B is attractive and sends perceived mating signals. So Person A becomes limerent and Person B becomes Limerent Object.

2. Person A's level of intensity and involuntary thought about B will depend on interpretation of B's interest.
3. If B is perceived as showing interest, A's happiness ensues and sustained involuntary thought diminishes to a potentially constant positive level.
4. If B is perceived as not interested, A yearns for reciprocation and intrusive thoughts increase and stay high.
5. Limerence is therefore B's actions as perceived by A, until B leaves or rejects, with even minimum attention able to sustain limerence for long periods of time, or B provides full reciprocation.

Tennov's (1999; 2005) theory of limerence might be complimented by alternative authors such as Baumeister & Wotman (1992) who focused on very specific facets of what is unfortunately a common limerent experience. In their book, *Breaking Hearts; Two sides of Unrequited Love*, they provide an unusual and unique perspective on the particular experience of unrequited love as seen from the experience of the *would-be lover* [i.e. LE] and the *rejecter* [i.e. LO]. Although they do not specifically address limerence as a form of love, the common experience of unrequited limerence makes the insights especially significant. The book focuses on the many incidences of unrequited feelings whereby LE may seek to both conceal their feelings to a LO of whom they may often know very little about, with some being near strangers or colleagues. The book follows the unfortunate trajectory of these experiences through to the actual rejection scene. In terms of limerence, unrequited experiences are often pivotal to the duration of the episode, since in theory, limerence should end at rejection. However, too often limerence sustains since, as Tennov (2005) points out, LE have the extraordinary ability to attempt to ignore or reinterpret what an objective observer might otherwise view as clear rejection. Additionally, the LO is often perceived as sending mixed signals and/or there are barriers involved (such as marriage), thereby prolonging uncertainty and intensity feeding the limerent experience.

Most recently, there have been a number of undergraduate and postgraduate publications (Pim, 2003; Hansen, 2006; Banker, 2010), along with academic articles (Clark, 2006), fiction (Hall, 2012) and even game design (Teck, 2011) using the limerence concept. Notably, Wakin & Vo (2008) recently responded to Tennov by providing a contemporary comprehensive review of the factors associated with limerent symptomology, grouping them in relation to the differential determination of limerence, being intrusive and obsessive thinking about the LO, replay and rehearsal, anxiety and self-consciousness, emotional dependence and impaired functioning. They state the new caveat (unlike Tennov) that the individual must be at least 18 years of age.

Intrusive and obsessive thinking regarding the LO
1. Thinking about LO more than anyone or anything else

2. Hard to avoid, reduce, stop focusing or concentrating on LO, even though there is voluntary control
3. Distractible such that relationships and responsibilities may be neglected
4. Constant, inflated positive or negative perceptions of LO cues

Replay and rehearsal
1. Highly sensitive to LO behavioural cues
2. Often constant replay of prior events and interactions regarding LO
3. Often constant anticipating/rehearsing events regarding future interactions with LO
4. Often constant imagining vivid experiences where LO reciprocates feelings and intentions
5. Often imagined experiences creates hope of reciprocation from LO, resulting in excessive and unreasonable behaviours/reactions
6. Often such actions compromise efficiency/ productivity

Anxiety and self-consciousness
1. Constant attempts to enhance physical appearance, behaviour, and attitude to appear more favourable to LO
2. Feelings of shyness, embarrassment and anxiety, with physiological symptoms (e.g. shortness of breath, perspiration, heart palpitations)
3. Heartache worsened with greater uncertainty and/or greater signs of rejection by LO

4. Social awkwardness in LO presence (e.g. stuttering, clumsiness)
5. Increased shyness, embarrassment, and anxiety in actual or imagined LO presence
6. Intense fear of being rejected by LO

Emotional dependence
1. Strong longing for reciprocation from LO
2. Depression and/or apprehension increase with greater uncertainty and/or signs of rejection by LO
3. Ecstasy increases with signs of reciprocation
4. Emotional lability
5. Longing for reciprocation increases with greater uncertainty of LO feelings
6. Longing for reciprocation increases with barriers

Impaired functioning
1. Relationships and responsibilities are neglected due to excessive thinking about LO
(Wakin & Vo, 2008)

In addition to reconsideration and grouping of symptomology, a further area of recent interest regards whether the limerent state appears to be linked to other psychological clinical conditions. Tennov (1999) herself recognised limerence as a condition of cognitive obsession whereby fantasy (albeit partly reality-based) was "intrusive and inescapable" (p40). However, Tennov (1999) also wanted to emphasise that while limerence was at variance with rationality and could reflect the state of stress, it should not be interpreted as "mental illness" (p90). She felt existing instability might cause limerence to show, but that it was not causational. She also noted that the LE, other than in terms of the state itself, were capable of being responsible and sane, with ex-LE having no permanent obsessive or distorted views toward their LO. Alternatively, more recent authors consider limerence as linked to forms of mental disorder, such as David Sack (2012) who emphasises the role of addiction and Wakin & Vo (2008) who consider the state as a combination of both addiction and Obsessive Compulsive Disorder.

In Wakin & Vo's (2008) I.D.R. model of limerence, the relationship between limerence and substance dependence and Obsessive Compulsive Disorder are cited, involving three functional components: *initiating force, driving forces,* and *resultant forces*. *Initiating force* regards the LE's initial feeling of longing for emotional reciprocation from the LO, which then progresses throughout the limerent episode. *Driving forces* regard the feeling of uncertainty and hope about the relationship with a fear of rejection. There is constant searching for *signs* of reciprocation with adjustments of behaviour in relation to perceived feedback from the LO, with such intensity that overanalysis and attempts at interpretation of the LO *signs* can become problematic thinking. Such thinking often involves replaying past interactions and rehearsing for potential future ones. Then the initial feeling of longing for emotional reciprocation manifests in the form of *driving forces*, ultimately creating a cycle "escalating the overall obsessive-compulsive and addictive reactions of Limerence" (p3).

Wakin & Vo (2008) suggest that following *driving forces*, *resultant forces* occur whereby the LE's mood becomes dependent on the LO, often involving labile states from extreme joy to despair, with a recognition by the LE that there is loss of control, such that the LE may consider attempts to remove the thinking or even close the relationship with the LO. However, due to the involuntary aspect of limerence, intentions are sometimes not able to be successfully carried out, leading to feelings of powerlessness and anxiety. Indeed, such feelings of anxiety may cause uncharacteristically awkward behaviours around the LO, such that compensatory behaviours are employed in order to gain the LO's approval and gauged as feedback leading to more uncertainty and anxiety. Finally, with involuntary limerent thinking ultimately resulting in other aspects of the LE's life being neglected, LE may experience feelings of shame and guilt, which the process of cognitive dissonance then facilitates justification by further inflating the significance of the LO, increasing the urgency for reciprocation. Thus the limerent cycle of "entrapment" (p4) completes.

For our part, further to addiction and Obsessive Compulsive Disorder, we suggest limerence may have similarities to other anxiety conditions including forms of Illness Anxiety Disorder, Hypochondria or *The Worried Well* in health contexts (Wick & Zanni, 2008). Specifically, in that along with addiction and Obsessive Compulsive Disorder, limerence may regard a form of *Free Floating Anxiety and Depression Temporarily Fixated.* In hypochondria, individuals that are predisposed toward worrying about health often display high general health anxiety, which is marked from time to time by being fixated by a specific health concern that then provides a focus for worry. During this time, other vaguer health anxieties become temporarily less salient. To this extent, we suggest that limerence may regard a similar process. Specifically, in limerence it may be that forms of anxious attachment are directed towards a misplaced attachment figure; the limerent object. The limerent trajectory that then plays out involves attempts to manage any induced separation anxiety and to emotionally connect, acquire validation and even attain versions of self-actualisation through the experience.

In terms of definitions, we concur that the negative attributes of the condition are significant, but we also propose the potential benefits of a limerent experience might be emphasised, in that, for many LE, the episode can become health inspiring, insightful, empowering and enlightening. Furthermore, unlike Tennov (1999) we recognise that the limerent experience primarily regards adoration and attachment that, though commonly, is not exclusively sexual. That is, limerence can be predominantly described as a feeling of adoration to a soul mate, rather than to a sexual partner per se. Note also here that the concept of a soul mate can regard a person that unsettles or instigates change, rather than being someone who is a savior. Thus for us, limerence involves the potential to journey towards a more authentic self (Willmott & Bentley, in press). We define limerence as:

"An involuntary, potentially inspiring state of adoration and attachment to a limerent object involving intrusive and obsessive thoughts, feelings and behaviours from euphoria to despair, contingent on perceived emotional reciprocation".

Notably, Tennov's original book dates back to 1979, and while she did update her work, her theoretical position remained largely unaltered. However, given current research on biology, neurochemistry, and brain imaging, we believe these additional considerations would now be welcome. Like Tennov, we do not offer a diagnostic tool or therapeutic framework for limerence, but would recommend that this could usefully be a focus for future work.

Therapeutic Case Study One

Tim was a successful man with a high flying career and a loving family. He was used to spending some time working with new staff, mentoring them, and was often invited to give presentations relating to his work. He was an important team leader. Tim came for psychotherapy because for the first time ever he felt he couldn't cope with life. He said that he had never expected that out of the blue he would feel obsessive about one of the new staff, that he felt they had a special link, that time spent away from her was time wasted. He also loved and valued his family, did not want to hurt them, did not want to "upset the boat" – he was struggling with both the overwhelming love and need for this other woman (LO) and the inability to think about the consequences. His rational mind knew he was being a "fool" but he also knew that LO was his soul mate, they were meant to be, LO was truly his significant other. He couldn't stop thinking about her, he didn't want to stop. Everything reminded him of their unique bond. The world was a brighter place. Quite apart from his emotional feelings being in turmoil, he was also suffering from cognitive dissonance – thinking/believing two completely opposing things about his family and the new, limerent situation, a real oxymoron. Therapy was based first in giving Tim time and space to express his feelings and thoughts, however contradictory they were. They were also very repetitive. As time went on and he talked and wept and talked more, we started to discuss alternative strategies to lessen his emotional pain. One strategy I used was: having heard Tim describe his friends and family and people he admired and/or liked, to ask for a description of the LO. It was clear to me that LO did not have many of the features in common with Tim's friends or family. And when I would ask, for example, how attractive he found people who would talk so much about themselves but not ask about nor listen to others, he would say that he didn't mix with such people as they were self-centered and not very nice. Tim is bright and knew why I was asking things, and would try and counter by saying "but…" and excusing LO for her traits.

Tim struggled, even though he found having a safe haven where he could speak freely very valuable. He had gotten to the point where he was desperate to move on and get back to being what he called "normal" again, to feel on an even level and not on an insane roller-coaster of emotions and thoughts. In his case, the humiliation he felt when he overheard some comments from LO, boasting to another girl about the hold she had on him and how he had recently offered to lend her a "stupid" book he'd enjoyed, and his sudden fear that his behaviour was making him notorious and a butt for unflattering jokes were helpful in supporting his desire to be free of LO and limerence. In fact, he felt deeply ashamed, appalled at what he might have done and might have gone on to do, desperate to escape from the whole situation, and very afraid that his family and friends might have gotten an idea of what went on. Actually, very little had gone on in one sense. Tim had smartened up, taken to spending more time in the coffee area as LO seemed to be there rather frequently to gossip with other women, and had become a friend – one among well over a hundred other people – on social media. He was now alternating between seeming paralysed with fear and being hysterically afraid of being exposed, all the time with the limerent thoughts darting in like arrows of fire to sear his being with false hopes.

Eventually, Tim regained his emotional composure. He made himself avoid places and situations where LO was likely to be, and while this seemed impossible initially, it did, over many months, become easier. He couldn't believe what he'd experienced. He felt humiliated, felt deeply bereaved and angry that she had not been the soul mate he had believed. He admitted he'd tried to bargain with a god in whom he did not believe that LO and he could become true friends, with no limerence. Then he admitted to feeling apathetic: what was the point of working, talking, being alive when he had lost the most significant opportunity in his life? About a year after he felt he was winning the fight to return to real life, he found, to his surprise, that he felt hardly any emotion at all on seeing the former LO and a man walking along with arms round each other. That relief did not last, but it did return, and as time went on, the relief lasted longer and occurred more frequently. Four years on from our first meeting, he seems back to being in balance with his world—family, work and leisure. He sees his ex-LO as the embers of a small fire, just enough warmth left to give an occasional tiny bit of comfort, and even this will probably fade more with time. He describes himself as "older, a bit wiser, a lot more aware and careful", but also not totally regretting the amazing emotional highs and inspiration he has experienced.

Therapeutic Case Study Two

Steve is young, in his twenties. He has had girlfriends, has had an even, pleasant life socially and at work. He values this as his childhood included emotional storms from his parents as they came to the end of their marriage and, when he was seven, on through a turbulent divorce. He says that school "saved" him as it was an oasis of calm compared to home.

But in the last two years, his happy life has been upset by what he sometimes calls his obsession. It started when one of the directors of his firm came to Steve's workplace to meet staff and then give a talk outlining plans and so on. Steve says he felt a jolt of electricity go through him at the meeting, he suddenly felt – he knew! - this man was the one to follow, the one who would understand, value, and appreciate Steve because, in spite of the differences in status and age, Steve just knew they were meant to be the sort of close buddies who hang out together and share everything. Steve says this is completely nonsexual, but he needs to be with this man to be the complete person he was meant to be, and is sure the same is true of the man, the LO.

Actual contact with the LO is rare, and they have never spoken one on one, but Steve is so certain they have that very special sort of bond; soul mates is a phrase he uses. But the effect of this on Steve and his life goes far beyond what might be called a crush. Steve is finding it really hard to focus on anything but thoughts of his LO, and this is making work stressful and social life complicated. He is constantly looking around when out and about in case he can get a glimpse of the LO even though this is unlikely. He is inattentive to others as his thoughts intrude, thoughts of the future, memories of when he has seen his LO, the significance of when the LO glanced in Steve's direction, plans for getting together with the LO, and so on. On the one hand, Steve says he realises he is fantasizing, but on the other hand, he then immediately talks about incidents at work where he just knows the LO has made contact via a third party, such as when a manager complimented Steve on work he'd recently done. When Steve is asked, "and how would the LO have done this?", he can't give a reasonable answer; he "just knows". And he "just knows" that glances toward himself are the signs that the LO returns these feelings, knows that they are a special couple, the most true of friends, friends on a deep and enduring level, friends with complete understanding of each other. Recently, after seeing the new James Bond movie, Steve described how he longed to protect his LO from attack, to show how he admires and adores him. Steve is also constantly looking on social media sites in case his LO has posted anything – and can be distraught when, of course, he sees he is not included in plans or activities, whether going to watch a game or meeting for a meal.

Steve says he spends 90% of his time in dark despair because he cannot find a way to be with his LO, his other half or soul mate. He talks sometimes about when, hypothetically, he is married, his wife and the LO's wife can spend time together while Steve and LO share their time, and how this time will be the most important and fulfilling.

When asked how long this has been going on, Steve looks distrait – it's been two years already. Steve's in a dark place, wanting to reclaim his life but also unable to face the mere thought of not seeing and being with his LO. Steve needs, in a confidential situation, to talk and talk about his LO, but the relief of doing this gives only a very temporary respite from being overwhelmed by his thoughts and feelings of hopelessness, true anguish. He is not ready even to contemplate the efforts he would have to make to free himself from what he has called his addiction, his limerence. However, he also says that the confidential and compassionate opportunity of therapy is worth doing now and may help him challenge his limerence in the future.

Gratitude and appreciation are given to "Tim" and "Steve" for this. Some details have been changed to protect the identity of "Tim", "Steve", and others.

Chapter 1

Foundations & Coexisting Conditions

Limerence can occur in differing degrees, from a variety of triggers and fuels. It appears that almost anyone can become limerent in terms of general demographic, probably being a reflection of the biological foundations of attraction. More controversial is the role that early life experiences may have had, such as those relating to early bonding, attachment and sensitivity of significant caregivers. Additionally, there could also be a role for individual differences including temperament and personalities or resilience, and lastly, limerence may be associated with coexisting disorders, such as anxiety and depression.

Biological Basis

Tennov (1999) stated, "it is hard to believe that we do not at least have built-in reactions in our basic natures that make the learning of significant strategies for biological survival (evolutionary development) easier than if culture operated on a proverbial blank slate" (p242). The blank slate or tabula rasa she referred to regards the early philosopher John Locke, who believed that children's development was largely dependent on the nurture of parents and societies (the nature nurture debate being a central discussion in any psychology classroom). Thus, Tennov (1999) believed that the limerent gene may be "well rooted — whatever our cultures and lifestyles — in the very nature of our humanness" (p242), given its common course and symptoms, similar experiences, and involuntary aspects. To this purpose, she was interested in the emerging field of Psychobiology, more likely now known as Cognitive Neuroscience.

Tennov (2005) suggested that the state of limerence was a "hardwired physio-psychological mechanism that is proximate to breeding and, therefore, to natural selection" (p268). Specifically, Tennov (1999) suggests that the limerent genetic transfer (along with other strategies) may have survived because the most consistent result of limerence is reproduction, commitment, nesting for shared ecstasy and for the rearing of children. She suggests that fear of rejection may take a part in prolonging the union processes (for example the average duration of 2 years being sufficient time to bear, birth and wean a child). She also suggests that limerence may function to free the young from prior parental attachments. In terms of the biology of attraction, Tennov (2005) noted that "It is probably controlled by the limbic system; it follows a rigid, unyielding, and predictable algorithmic pattern" (p262), with the algorithmic pattern that she described having been set out in her law of limerence. However, Tennov notes that "although limerence may well be an adaptation selected during evolutionary development, it is not necessarily an aid to reproductive success in the contemporary environment" (Tennov, 2005. p264).

The limbic brain that Tennov (2005) referred to involves structures from reptilian evolution creating a *border* or *edge* as a subsequent division between reptilian and mammalian life, as termed by neuroanatomist, Paul Broca in 1879 (Schiller, 1992). The outer neocortex represents facets such as language, cognition, and the conscious part of the brain (Bradshaw, 1990). According to Lewes, Amini and Lannon (2001) in mammals this feature created a novel response of the "intimate mental embrace of love" (p50), but they also note that the brain is "fragmented and inharmonious, and to some degree composed of players with competing interests" (p31). Lewes et al (2001) go on to describe how in limbic regulation a loop-back system occurs whereby varied physiological responses are constantly fine-tuned, with this system potentially able to keep synchronised including coping with external stimuli. However, in extreme or stressful cases, a second person such as a LO can alter processes such as hormone levels, immunology, etc., resulting in a state of unbalance.

Fisher (2004) concurs with the biological foundations of romantic love as she sets out in her book *Why We Love; The Nature and Chemistry of Romantic Love.* She cites three key brain chemicals involved with love being: dopamine, norepinephrine (also known in the UK as noradrenaline) and serotonin, which, though varying in their concentrations and interactions, she suggests are crucial to obsessive and passionate love. Specifically, dopamine is associated with selective attention, motivation, and goal focused activities. Thus, a love [LO] can become the new centre for focus, negative traits are downplayed, and the love [LO] will be seen as the *only one*, which is in keeping with dopamine's associations with learning new stimuli. Additionally, dopamine is associated with excitation generally and is likely implicated in many of the physiological symptoms such as increased heart rate and breathing, through to broader persistence, sexual desire, or anxiety and fear responses. Norepinephrine has been associated with common experiences in romantic love including excitation, sleeplessness, lost appetite, as well as improved memory for new stimuli, though its effects are more varied regarding specific brain locations. Whereas serotonin compounds may be associated with the propensity to excessively think about or ruminate on the chosen love [LO], with these chemicals reducing under the influence of the rise in dopamine and norepinephrine.

According to Tallis (2004), phenylethylamine (an amphetamine-like compound) is also implicated in love, raising mood and energy, as are endorphins (opium-like substances), which are involved in the regulation of appetite, pain, pleasure, and sex hormones. But of the brain chemicals so far, it is dopamine that has been more thoroughly mapped in romantic love. Through fMRI brain scanning, Fisher (2004) was able to identify specific brain regions involved in romantic love, including the caudate nucleus with its charge of dopamine. This region at the brain's center is known as the primitive reptilian brain or R-complex, due to its evolutionary foundations and is associated with attention, reward, and learning. Also implicated was the ventral tegmental area of the brain, again associated with reward, as well as dopamine production and distribution. She postulates that norepinephrine and serotonin, together with the brain's prefrontal cortex, are likely to be involved in romantic love.

Along with romantic attraction and the chemistry involved, Fisher (2004) also describes the specific and differentiated role of lust or the mating drive as largely involving the hormone testosterone for both men and women. She notes romance and lust are not unrelated, since dopamine (related to the former) can stimulate testosterone (regarding the latter), as can norepinephrine, albeit with caveats of dosage and interactions. Moreover, she notes that while romance might stimulate lust, lust may not necessarily stimulate romance, but interestingly, romance does seem to relate to attachment.

Attachment

Just as Fisher (2004) proposed a biological foundation for romantic attraction and lust, she also suggested a third factor, attachment, involving the hormones oxytocin and vasopressin (also known in the UK as ADH), which are released mainly by the pituitary gland. Indeed, she viewed romantic attraction, lust, and attachment as being systems with multiple purposes. Most recently, the neural correlates of long-term intense love and attachment have also been mapped showing that for some individuals the reward-value facets apparent in new love may be sustained with a long-term partner, along with the involvement of brain systems implicated in attachment and pair-bonding (Acevedo, Aron, Fisher & Brown, 2012). Others suggest the potentially long reaching biological components of attachment such as those related to the *limbic bond,* with Lewis et al (2001) stating "If someone's relationships today bear a troubled imprint, they do so because an influential relationship left its mark on a child's mind" (p177).

In terms of specific chemicals, oxytocin is associated with stimulating early bonding, but also, it seems, with adult pairing attachments. Oxytocin is made mostly in the hypothalamus, as well as ovaries and testes, and is associated with the birth process and breast-feeding. Indeed, together, oxytocin and vasopressin release is also involved in sexual intercourse—for example, at orgasm, the former increases in women and the latter in men (Fisher, 2004). Indeed, according to Tallis (2004), "Oxytocin is the closest science has come to identifying the chemical substrate of love" (p230).

The idea that children are biologically predisposed to attach to caregivers to maximise their survival chances was largely developed by the psychologist John Bowlby in the 1960s, based on the ideas of ethological theory including imprinting, a process in animals akin to attachment (Lorenz, 1952). Tennov (1999) herself recognised that there were similarities between imprinting and the limerent experience, specifically involving the role of involuntary and unconscious factors. She specifically notes the case of "negative imprinting" (p251) in consideration to the evidence from kibbutz children whereby early intimacy (that is living together under the age of 5) apparently interfered with the subsequent incidence of limerence later in life, in spite of parental influence to the contrary (Talmon,

1964). Thus, Tennov also notes the role imprinting may play for mate selection, including guarding against incest, since genetic inbreeding risks genetic weakness.

Bowlby's (1969) original theory of attachment described how, through attachment, children develop lasting emotional ties and create an *internal working model of attachment,* which is available thereafter in reference for future relationships. He proposed four attachment phases being; (1) *pre-attachment* (0-6 weeks) innate behaviours such as crying call caregivers resulting in comforting interaction, (2) *attachment in the making* (6 weeks-6/8 months) preference to special caregivers, interactions include smiling, babbling with the baby, developing expectations about the caregivers' ability to meet needs and trustworthiness, (3) *clear cut attachment* (8 months-1.5 years) baby prefers regular caregivers and may experience separation anxiety if parted. The mother becomes a secure base for exploration of world, (4) *reciprocal relationships* (1.5/2 years plus) toddlers cognitive and language abilities increase such that wider strategies can be employed for maintaining closeness with caregivers and separation anxiety can decrease. In prolonged separation, Bowlby (1980) noted that eventually detachment can occur.

The theory of attachment was developed further by using a procedure called the Strange Situation, which investigated the concept of the caregiver as a secure base by focusing on the separation/reunion of infants-caregivers (Ainsworth, 1967; Ainsworth, 1973). Using this procedure, attachment types were categorised into being either *securely* attached, notably they are pleased to see the caregiver return or are easily comforted, or *insecurely* attached, which was subtyped into *anxious resistant/ambivalent, anxious avoidant* or later a further category was added—*disorganised* (Main & Solomen, 1990). Infants categorised as *resistant/ambivalent* may be clingy, cry and difficult to comfort, whereas *avoidant* infants largely ignore the caregiver. Lastly, *disorganised/disoriented* infants have confused or contradictory behaviour.

Varied subsequent research has shown that attachment categories may be relatively enduring (especially where there are no intervening significant life events such as divorce in families) and predictive of later psychology, behaviours, and relationships (Lucas-Thompson & Clarke-Stewart, 2007; Simpson, Collins, Tran & Haydon, 2007). Also that there are numerous factors that are influential to attachment, particularly parental sensitivity (Ainsworth, Blehar, Waters & Wall, 1978), critical or sensitive periods (Kreppner, Rutter, Becket, Castle, Colvert, 2007), the ability to form multiple attachments (Schaffer & Emerson, 1964; Lewis et al, 2001), social economic status (Nievar & Becker, 2007), as well as broader cultural differences (Takahashi, 1986; Rothbaum, Pott, Azuma, Miyake & Weisz, 2000).

Relevant to LE is the theme that those who are or have become familiar with attachment theory often believe that they were *insecurely anxiously* attached. The relevance of these attachments categories being clarified by Lewis et al (2001) when they note that "the brains of insecurely attached children react to provocative events with an exaggerated outpouring of stress hormones and neurotransmitters" (p211), with the over-reactivity enduring into adulthood risking associated anxieties and depression. Clearly without the ability to go back and categorise specific LE as infants, it is not possible to be sure in which category they would have been placed. However, what is interesting is that where psychologists have attempted to review adults' own views of their perceived early attachments in retrospect (Main, Kaplan & Cassidy, 1985), they have tended to confirm that secure or insecure categories can persist through generations (Benoit & Parker, 1994).

George, Kaplan & Main (1984) categorised adult attachments into *autonomous/secure* involving a balanced recall of positive and negative features or *insecure* with subtypes of *dismissing, preoccupied,* and *unresolved/disorganised*. Given these categories, LE might cite their view again for *insecure* attachments since often they report that a particular early caregiver or life event interrupted or damaged their attachments in some way. Specifically, of the select LE cases available, there are examples relating to childhood experiences of specific parental behaviours as well as life events such as adoption, divorce, and death. Indeed, there are LE who describe how their attachments have included a state of unpleasantness or pain. Some LE come to realise that their LO represents or is part of a projection of past unresolved or broken relationships associated with attachment (projection being a defence mechanism whereby internal states are ascribed, often unconsciously, to others - Freud, 1936). Interestingly, the role of misplaced attachments becomes a particular theme pertinent to those LE who have experienced rejection or starvation in a limerent episode, but are finding it difficult to disengage from their LO even in the case of increasingly humiliating interactions.

Given the view that the pattern of perceived attachment and subsequent bonding to present or future children can be relatively enduring, for LE, it may be for this reason, and others, that attachment issues become a key consideration. Indeed, LE seem to want to contemplate their own early attachments with a view to gaining better understanding or to even addressing potential issues with the persons concerned (e.g. their own mother/father). Certainly, LE describe a desire to, wherever possible, alter the pervasive cycle of insecure attachments that they themselves may be implicated in with their own children. LE might concur and seek to achieve the proposition regarding their own current attachment relationships as those that ideally would rather involve unconditional positive regard (Rogers, 1994) and sensitivity (Ainsworth et al, 1978). Moreover, LE whom are parents to grown-up children might concur with Halpern (1979) who usefully advocates that it is possible to be "attached by caring, not strings....A loving separateness. It is what a relationship... can be" (p223).

Additionally, Baumeister & Wotman (1992) suggests that attachment theory is a useful perspective for unrequited love [limerence] in that it tracks a path of rejection. That is, it explains the biologically-driven behaviour of *would-be lovers* [LE] as following a predictable set of stages (Bowlby, 1969; 1973; 1980), being: distress about the other's absence, followed by despair, depression, and sadness, then at some point, detachment involving indifference or even avoidance. Notably, Baumeister & Wotman (1992) suggest that attachment theory might also give insight to the uncomfortable position of the *rejecters* [LO], in that it explains why they will find it hard and upsetting to reject love.

Lastly, it must be noted that the specific role that attachment might play in the limerence experience is complicated particularly by the fact that many associations may regard a very young age, possibly being preverbal, as potentially subject to biased recollection or childhood amnesia (Hayne, 2004). Furthermore, in addition to any biological foundations for limerence, be they romance, lust, or based on attachment, an interplay of states, traits, or personal circumstances may also be relevant.

Limerent Demographics

LE range across a wide range of demographic. Indeed, Tennov (2005) suggested that she could see no relationship to "level of education, gender, occupation, philosophy" (p14). The experience can happen to anyone, it seems, is often unexpected, and can be welcome or unwelcome at the start. It may occur at almost any age, to people who are single, married, or have SO.

Age

In terms of the incidence of limerence with age, Tennov (2005) suggested limerence is most probable in youth and early adulthood since both are best proximal to physical attractiveness as an indication of good health and genetic fitness, but she placed no upper or lower age restrictions as such. However Wakin & Vo (2008) set their symptomology for limerence to individuals above the age of 18. Current online LE specific sites contain the full range of ages, with many below 18 years. However, to what extent this is an accurate demographic is difficult to say. There may in fact be significantly more or less under 18 limerent online users than reported since there could be an inclination toward falsifying age online and/or younger internet users may prefer utilising alternative terms and support sites such as those that are more commonly related to youth (e.g. sites regarding *crush* or *infatuation*). Either way, as yet we do not know whether limerence is in any way age specific.

Gender

In regard to gender, Tennov (1999) noted that there were no overall differences in limerence, but that there may be differences in reporting bias and how easily or how often limerence occurs. For example, she found that while limerence affects both men and women as seen in general description evidence, men were less likely to express their limerence in the form of questionnaires, probably given cultural sex role expectations such as female emotional dependency. Also, she noted the incidence of limerence frequently with middle-aged professional men and in women that stay at home with their children. With the latter, she suggested the incidence probably reflecting the issues of isolation, such that any "desirable man who pays regular attention to them may become a potential LO". (p200). Additionally, she suggested that men may be more successful in limerence for longer (that is have less negative outcomes), given that women are seen to lose their physical attractiveness as they age, thus she suggests women may presumably be more easily inclined to lose hope sooner.

In terms of gender orientation, Tennov (1999) reports cases of *homolimerence,* that is where there are incidences of gay or lesbian limerence experiences but not of *bi-experiences*, though she notes there were too few accounts in her initial interviews to usefully generalise. She noted a difference in *homolimerence* between gender, in that there was less promiscuity reported in the lesbian respondents, as opposed to the gay, in keeping with other sources of statistics, and that limerence occurring between younger to older woman may reflect a form of "hero worship" (Tennov, 1999. p216). It must be noted of course that, particularly in Tennov's original writing, her accounts reflect the sex and gender experiences and roles such that it was in her time. So for example, though still it is often the case today that, when a family unit does involve a man and women, disproportionately it is the women that are likely to be at home with younger children. It is also the case that present day family units are varied and any isolation aspects experienced by a partner who stays at home have potentially changed by many factors such as flexi working and virtual social networking to name but two. Certainly, in current online LE communities, there appears to be as many female as male LE and accounts from different gender orientations including heterosexual, lesbian, gay, and bi-experiences, irrespective of their roles within families.

Indeed, when considering the factors of *who becomes limerent to whom*, it may first be prudent to first re-revisit Tennov's (1979) original proposition, that limerence includes sexual attraction, that is that the LO is potentially a sexual partner of "the preferred gender" (Tennov, 2005. p10). Rather, it may be necessary to emphasis the caveat that some LE do not regard sexual attraction, indeed some may not even like their LO! In relation to sexual attraction, even Tennov (1999) herself, did find a few incidences where there was apparently no inclination toward sex and certainly the experiences of even the current select LE would support that finding. Thus, while it can be noted that there are often LE who report a limerent experience that then becomes the initiation of their future gender orientation (be it heterosexual, lesbian, gay or bi), there are others who report that their LO choice does not subsequently involve any such relevance to their sexual attraction. That is a heterosexual can report having a same sex LO and a homosexual can report having a cross sex LO etc. Now, while it may be that others might suggest they are in some sort of version of denial, these LE might instead report that their limerence is specific to the target LO, less because of sexual attraction and more because of some other trigger, fundamental need or feeling of being a soul mate. For example, *"Right from the start there was something about her that was bewitching. I've spent ages thinking it through, and I know it is not sexual. But still I want to be close to her. I need to be with her." (Undisclosed Author)*. These experiences are too many to be ignored, and indeed, it is recognised that the triggers for a potential LO are varied and complicated, such that it is entirely possible that the role of gender and sexual attraction may be a relatively consistent, but not invariable, selection feature.

Similarly, some LE report not liking their LO (let alone finding them sexually attractive!). This seems to be the case particularly for LE who have fallen into limerence without knowing much about the LO, so that the limerence escalated faster than any incoming knowledge with any new knowledge being liable to be largely ignored or played down. Such LE can describe and indeed joke about their incompatibility to their LO and to how they sometimes have to work hard to remove the things the LO does or says from their consciousness when it is at odds with their own values and sensitivities.

Triggers

Fisher (2004) describes how we tend to fall in love using a form of map, which is made up of biological foundations and preferences of attraction, as well as early life role models and later romantic experiences. In relation to limerence specifically, Tennov (1999) suggested that a potential LO may be "anyone who meets a certain rough criteria" (p107), generally including similarity of ethnic, racial and social economic status. She also noted that factors related to age and physical attractiveness were relevant, all affected by culture even in regard to fashion (Tennov, 1999). However, regarding culture and expectations, she noted that limerence appears to "enjoy a certain immunity to influence" (p224), such that culture can shift conceptions of beauty but only to a limited degree. Notwithstanding these factors, in the end she notes "persons across a wide range of physical appearances secure mates" (Tennov, 1999. p254).

LO may be varied indeed, and to this extent, it is often remarked that one's LO appears a less desirable choice to anyone else. That is, not all LO are classically beautiful and luckily (or unluckily) there are plenty of potential LO to go around. Notably, some LO are selected with no initial visual cues at all, with accounts of LE recognizing the episode was triggered virtually such as by prior e-mail correspondence or online gaming contact, thus the process was well underway before any visual attractiveness considerations emerged. The triggers then, can be less likely to do with a particular LO, and more to do with a state of *readiness* of the LE, primarily. So there is a complicated (and possibly part unconscious) state including readiness, an underlying state of present mind and personal circumstance of the LE, as well as the coincidences of meeting with the LO and how each interaction develops, as well as triggers associated with an individual LO such as perceived attractiveness and gestures ascribed to the LO (for those where this information is available), to name but a few potential factors involved.

Interestingly, whatever the initial triggers were, often LE that do have initial visual contact with their LO, in retrospect have an uncanny ability to reflect and identify potential behaviour gestures that they believe their LO made that they come to regard as pivotal to the limerent episode commencing. For example, LE recall an unusual or intense eye contact, smile, or accidental touch from the LO that they feel started their limerent episode. Some describe the trigger as the way that their LO spoke to them or even an eyebrow raise on first meeting (this gesture is ambiguous because it can signal recognition in greeting, surprise or attraction). Some LE in retrospect suggest that their LO reminds them of another person that they know in some way (e.g. they look or act like a sibling or friend in some respect). Certainly, some LE are able to recognise in retrospect that their LO was comparatively more attractive (with classical markers including symmetry of features/body or clear skin), or suited some unmet need, had a skill, knowledge, or power that was desired and therefore seductive (Tallis, 2004; Baumeister & Wotman, 1992).

Personal circumstances of the LE might also play a part in limerence triggers since even those that say they were in happy marriages or with SO, sometimes review their situation and, in retrospect, recognise there may have been some holes in the current relationships, or that there were some personal boundary issues that were not ideal. In these cases, themes of loneliness, complacency, boredom, or being trapped in the existing relationship emerge, such that LE may have (unconsciously or not) been reaching out to others. Having said that, there are some LE who continue to consider themselves in a positive relationship and state of mind when the limerent episode was triggered and it is these LE who often regard the event as most unexpected and unwelcome since they then might have less an identifiable purpose for the LO or likely insight from the experience that is usefully transferable. For example, *"I had in no way planned for it, and I had no purpose for her [my LO] in my life. I guess it was unwanted and inconvenient for all three of us - my wife, my LO, and me!" (Undisclosed Author).* Indeed, such LE might warn that it can be dangerous to then embark on a process and feel obliged to locate potential fault findings within the current relationship when there really may be few or none. Rather, it might be best placed to note that happy relationships (with SO or spouses) are not in themselves sufficient to inoculate from limerence (Tennov, 1999; Fisher, 2004).

Interestingly, Fisher (2004) suggests that any state of emotional arousal may involve an increased vulnerability toward love, given the potential increase in dopamine levels. However, for the majority of LE, their state of mind at the time the limerent episode started tended to be negative, rather than positive. For instance, LE might describe being at a low point including being particularly stressed, anxious and depressed or having high sensitivity or a low self-esteem for some reason. To this extent, limerence can serve as escapism and distraction, with the LO as the *escape route*. In the common case of preexisting anxiety, it may be that limerence comes to represent a form of *free floating anxiety temporarily fixated* and, as such, there is some comfort to be found in isolating a particular target (the LO) along with any pleasant feelings and thoughts limerence affords. Similarly, *depression* is a very common theme, and mostly when

LE recognise a state of preexisting anxiety or depression prior to the limerent experience, they are most loath to desist from the episode, even when trapped in a phase of starvation and the associated unpleasantness. In some ways, there appears to be a preference for a state of mind where there was at least some hopefulness or *euphoric recall* as part of the experience, as opposed to a disturbing, empty, featureless, and pointless state of anxiety or low mood. Certainly overall, there appears to be a general reluctance to end the limerent episode if it will involve potentially returning to any identified less favourable preexisting state of mind.

Relationship of Limerence to Other Traits

Along with states of mind as potential triggers for the occurrence of a limerence episode, some suggest there may be more permanent traits or underlying predispositions, such as avoidance, codependency, possessiveness and compulsiveness, along with the incidence of anxiety and depression, dissociative identity and post-traumatic stress disorder (Horowitz, 1986). Similarly, there is the incidence described of the potential connection between limerence and language and communication disorders, such as Asperger's Syndrome, whereby abilities to correctly interpret social interaction with a potential LO may be particularly impaired.

Notably, however, few LE might concur that there is any significant connection to delusional disorders, such as de Clerambault Syndrome or Erotomania, as per the Diagnostic Statistical Manual for Mental Disorders (4th ed.; DSM IV TR; American Psychiatric Association, 2000), which mostly relate to a delusion that a high status person or stranger is secretly in love with them. Indeed, to date, limerence is not detailed in the Diagnostic Statistical Manual for Mental Disorders (5th ed.; DSM-5; American Psychiatric Association, 2013). However, it could be that Separation Anxiety Disorders such as Childhood Separation Anxiety Disorder (4th ed.; DSM IV,TR; American Psychiatric Association, 2000) and/or Adult Separation Anxiety Disorder (5th ed.; DSM-5; American Psychiatric Association, 2013) might now be useful concepts for understanding Limerence, since "both [disorders] share characteristics of recurrent excessive distress when anticipated or experienced separation regarding a major attachment figure occurs, which causes impairment to functioning" (Willmott & Bentley, in press).

Tennov's (1999) own belief was that limerence was not related to personality, nor was it a mental illness, stating instead that it was a "normal and nonpathological condition" (Tennov, 2005. p17); however, she did agree that it bore similarities to addiction. Indeed, LE often describe the thought of recovery from their limerent experience as if they were attempting recovering from any other form of addiction. For example, *"limerence is like a drug, like giving up cigarettes, you just have to stop and know that it's going to be hard. Tips for stopping then might include: putting away anything that could trigger a memory of your LO, followed by planning and preparing to stop seeing them, including selecting a date, avoiding them and then expecting it to be difficult, so forgiving any relapses." (Undisclosed Author).*

David Sack, an addiction expert, considers the addictive qualities of limerence in relation to its biological foundations and suggests, "in much the same way that changes in the brain cause drug addicts to feel an intense, all-consuming draw to get and use drugs, limerence can drive people to extremes in the pursuit of the object of their affection". Thus, he further notes that many LE "chase that lovesick feeling at the expense of their careers, families and health". He notes how some behaviours may even become dangerous, requiring professional treatment such as counseling or 12-step work such as those used as a foundation framework in Alcoholics Anonymous (Sack, 2012).

Wakin & Vo (2008) go further to propose an interface between limerence, substance dependence, and Obsessive Compulsive Disorder. In relation to addiction, they suggest limerence involves similarities of attributes including the roles of tolerance, physical symptomology, compulsive behaviour, lack of control, impairment, and distress. For example, in limerence, tolerance is experienced in that there is a longing for emotional reciprocation from the LO in order to create or maintain a state of desired happiness, with physical symptoms occurring in occasions of withdrawal from the LO (e.g. physical pain in the chest and abdominal regions, sleep disturbance, irritability, and depression). Additionally, there is a pattern of compulsive behaviour involving increased planning for access to the LO, with LE being unable to control or reduce the need for their LO despite recognizing the negative effects, including the impairment and distress being caused. In relation to the interface between limerence and Obsessive Compulsive

Disorder, it is suggested that both share an undercurrent of anxiety especially focused on the potential rejection from the LO. The LE may engage in repetitive thoughts or behaviours to dissipate anxiety, which are time-consuming and therefore can interfere with the LE ability to function normally.

However, while Wakin & Vo (2008) cite addiction and Obsessive Compulsive Disorder as potentially integral, they also warn that they can be an oversimplification of limerence. Since the goal of limerence is emotional reciprocation, with feedback dependent on an LO for whom behaviour may change and may be prompted to change in response to the behaviour of the LE. As such, "defining limerence as an obsessive compulsive addiction or an addictive OCD would be a failure to consider the nature of the interpersonal nuances between L [LE] and LO and how they compound to complicate the overall process of limerence" (p7).

Lastly, in terms of the potential biology involved, Fisher (2004) describes both the role of Obsessive Compulsive Disorder and addiction. Specifically, she cites the brain chemical dopamine as associated with romantic attraction or love, noting that elevated levels are associated with all major addictions. Additionally, she notes that, in love, the brain's mesolimbic reward system is activated by dopamine and suggests love includes classic symptoms of addiction such as tolerance, withdrawal, and relapse. Similarly, low levels of the brain chemical serotonin have been implicated in romantic attraction and love and also in cases of Obsessive Compulsive Disorder. Indeed, the latter may have biological and evolutionary foundations with both parental and romantic love (Leckman, Mayes, Feldman, Evans, King & Cohen, 1999: Leckman & Mayes, 1999).

Interactional Effects

Whatever the biological foundations of love and its variances, many authors state that the relationship is probably hugely varied and interactional (Fisher, 2004), with countless other processes involved, including dynamic systems such as memory (Lewis et al, 2001; Lewis, 2005). Overall, Fisher (2004) suggests that the chemistry of lust can trigger attachment and the chemistry of attachment can trigger love, but the relationship is complex, such that attachment can dampen lust as can be evidenced in many a long-term relationship. Similarly, the chemistry of attachment can reduce romance, again as many a long-term romance can demonstrate! For the lucky, both romance and attachment persist. However, of most important relevance to the limerence experiences is perhaps the proposition that desire, romance and attachment can co-occur in any combination (Fisher, 2004) and that it may be targeted to more than one person (this being unfortunate given many societies common inclination toward exclusive long-term relationships). Specifically, that it is entirely possible, whatever your age, gender, or personal circumstance to be in a state of lust and romance [and adoration and attachment - limerence] for one person, even if you are in a conventional attachment (e.g. marriage or with a SO) with someone else!

Also, it should be noted that while there are examples from LE where there may be a predisposition of states or traits associated with limerence, it must also be useful to consider that predispositional factors are also likely to be highly complex and interactional such that there may equally be incidences where individuals do not succumb to limerence. For example, developmental psychology recognises that children with positive personal qualities, easygoing temperament, ability to adapt to change, and a close relationship with at least one parent and other adult may best overcome disadvantage (Rutter, 2006; Masten, 2007). So it may well be that these children and others who, in spite of having a number of predispositions, could remain resilient to limerence? Thus early bonding and attachment issues alone may not inevitably produce misplaced and inappropriate limerent attachments of the future.

Furthermore, while it is highly likely that LE are able to accurately recognise key predispositional factors toward limerence, it is also worth noting that some LE report that, in their desperation to look back and identify causes, they often tend to make salient any events immediately preceding the episodes start, rather than other contributory causes, be they less obvious or multifaceted and interactional. The phenomenon of identifying salient and sometimes erroneous causes immediately preceding unexpected events has long been recognised as a common one in regard to health threats (Petrie & Weinman, 1997). To this end and in avoidance of this tendency, LE recognise it is useful to take some time to reflect and review past and present factors that may be involved in any limerent episode, a process that might usefully be done alone or with external support. Either way, this would likely be a process best done given insight and understanding of the complexity of the limerent experience.

Chapter 2

Individual & Social Effects of Limerence

Limerence can play out as an algorithm or involve varied events and outcomes such as rejection, starvation, minimum attention, full reciprocation, or consummation, as well as transference (Tennov 1999; 2005). There is also a complicated role for limerence in friendships. In all cases and scenarios, there will be LO who have done nothing to encourage it, or those in which the LO (unconsciously or not) has encouraged the LE in order perhaps to enjoy the attention or power this brings. Such an LO might come from among virtual strangers, friends, work colleagues, or even other people's SO or spouses.

Rejection
According to Fisher (2004), romantic love can often unfortunately come to involve rejection, which contains its own biological components. Rejection is marked by phases of *protest* followed by *resignation and despair*, involving such issues as sleeplessness, weight loss, and rumination. Protest is related to the *separation anxiety* of attachment theories whereby the brain activates stress responses such as the synthesizing and releasing of the stress hormone cortisol. Unfortunately and ironically, short-term stress has also been associated

with triggering the production of the key chemicals associated with romantic love, i.e. increased dopamine and norepinephrine levels and reduced serotonin, with longer-term stress potentially plummeting all three chemicals toward depression.

Most recently, Fisher, Brown, Aron, Strong & Mashek (2010) note how rejection is associated with gain, loss, and craving linked to emotional regulation of the brain including the ventral tegmental area, ventral striatum, medial and lateral orbitofrontal/prefrontal cortex, and cingulate gyrus, with Eisenberger & Lieberman (2004) suggesting that the anterior cingulate cortex is the key regarding the physical-social pain overlap. Indeed, the biological processes and potentially pathological effects of emotional stress can potentially be health threatening as described in broken heart syndrome (Stress Cardiomyopathy, Takotsubo Syndrome, or Transient Left Ventricular Systolic Dysfunction), although this occurrence is rarely fatal except in the case of physical stressors and mostly affects older women (Wittstein, 2007).

Baumeister & Wotman (1992) suggest two common paths toward likely rejection include those regarding the problem of *falling upward* and/or platonic intimacy. Firstly, it seems that, in terms of marriage partners, people tend to pair off in similar attractiveness, education, and intelligence, but in attraction, there is a tendency toward rejection because there is a mismatch between attractiveness and desirability with the *would-be lover* [LE] *falling upward* toward a *rejecter* [LO] that is unlikely to reciprocate. While rational decision making at the start might avoid the scenario, they note there is often irrationality in love's start and a tendency of many to overestimate their own attractiveness. Secondly, there is a path to rejection through friendship, where the physical attractiveness is less salient and over time platonic intimacy unfolds. This moves one to the role of *would-be lover* [LE] and the other to *rejecter* [LO]. Once initiated, they note how the *would-be lover* [LE] has the option of actively trying to *win* love in a *high-stakes gamble* or passively giving up, whereas the *rejecter* [LO] is forced either to play along or reject (both being unpleasant outcomes). So for the former, issues of self-esteem become relevant; while for the latter, central issues regarding guilt and justification become relevant, thus representing a potential threat to [LO] perceived *morality*. They note how the *would-be lover* [LE] has the advantage of many social *scripts* (from poems to songs) with which to express their predicament, as against the experience of the *rejecter* [LO] who is largely *scriptless*, except possibly for the advice of *local peers*.

Baumeister & Wotman (1992) also note how often there can be mixed messages since the *rejecter* [LO] may have had initial feelings of being mildly flattered, then guilt, then confusion and annoyance, through to possibly anger, and repulsion, while still struggling not to hurt the other's feelings. They suggest there is an *emotional crossfire,* whereby both parties may have experienced positive and negative states in retrospect, in the final analysis with the latter more prevalent. They suggest that often the situation is complicated by a *conspiracy of silence*, whereby both parties dread the rejection experience. Then, even when the rejection does come, it can be somewhat unclear or less than honest in an attempt to cause least hurt and avoid an unpleasant scene, such that the message fails to motivate the unfortunate *would-be lover* [LE] to desist in their pursuit.

Painful though it is, Tennov (1999) was an advocate for rejection in limerence. She believed LO have responsibilities of an *ethical kind* toward the LE in order to help them *diminish the pain* and avoid any *suffocating attention toward themselves* or even danger. Indeed, Baumeister & Wotman (1992) might concur with the approach, especially since they recognise that the *would-be lover* [LE] may be so caught up in their needs that they fail to consider the *rejecter's* [LO] position, such that it is, in fact, the rejecter who has more insight (and therefore, potentially more ability to act rationally). They go on to suggest that the insight of the *rejecters* [LO] is akin to having more empathy and understanding, which could presumably be helpful to marshal when formulating the rejection plan. However, in regard to empathy and understanding, Tennov (1999) might warn the LO against offering any forms of friendly compassion since the risk is that it may be perceived as hope to the LE, which will not help end the limerence.

During this time in particular, LO may be perceived by the LE as being *cold, deceptive, and exploitative*. Certainly, there are accounts of LO actively hiding from the LE or engaging in the most minimal conversation and running off at first opportunity. Baumeister & Wotman (1992) note that clearly this is a particularly awkward time for both parties and, in truth, both might look back on such times with unpleasant regard. For the LO, there is the unwanted experience of having to witness the distress they may have caused, together with a motive of self-preservation in attempting to avoid any scene the LE might make. For the LE, there is a necessary adjustment into heartbreak to be made, a process which might be best if not played out in front of the perpetrator of the pain. However, in spite of all these difficulties and likely unpleasantness associated with rejection, Tennov (1999) is clear that an LO should best do "whatever is necessary to eliminate any trace of hope". For example, by stating "I am not limerent toward you", "I don't wish to be limerent toward you", "I am limerent about it _____" (p267).

While Baumeister & Wotman (1992) do offer a useful overview of unrequited love, which may be very insightful to the limerent experience, one area where the focus might be somewhat different in limerence is in regard to the unexpected occurrence and timing of rejection that appears to be prevalent in the limerent trajectory. That is, notwithstanding Tennov's (1999) proposition that rejection is a constant fear, some LE recount a type of denial at the height of the limerent episode in which they are actually awaiting sure reciprocation rather than being expectant of rejection. The extent of that denial is shown when rejection comes as there is often a strong sense of shock. For example, *"From the moment I met him, I lit up, I was friendly and happy. I felt that we were connected in some way. The feeling was so intense I thought he felt it too (though, of course, I never mentioned it to him or anyone else). But then, one day at the finish of a [work related] meeting, he said, "I would appreciate it if you stopped flirting because I've started dating a girl who works on the next floor". I had no idea that I had been offending him with my adoration. I then felt 100% to blame, since I realised that previously at no point had he been anything other than indifferent and polite to me. Bizarrely, for the next few weeks, I stayed happy (I now know this was shock), but then he increasingly showed disrespect toward me. Eventually, like a drip feed, realization took place and I began to experience the humiliation, shame, etc. and I fell... and I fell... and I fell... it took ages to finally stop the pain"* (Undisclosed Author).

Furthermore, the limerence trajectory would probably put an emphasis on how, even when rejection is given, LE can still persist in their feelings toward their LO, often referring to feelings of being *stuck* or *trapped*. As discussed in the previous chapter, some LE make the direct link between feeling stuck, trapped, or unable to let go and the recognition that they have (unconsciously or not) acted out a relationship with their LO that they later come to recognise as pertaining to another figure in their lives, particularly ones associated with earlier attachments and bonding. Indeed, it is possible that there may be multiple attachment figures implicated within a limerent episode. The LO as a misplaced or inappropriate attachment may be pivotal in the related significant theme of just wanting to *talk or connect* in some way, even post rejection, in spite of the knowledge that it is unwelcome and one-sided. Interestingly, such difficulties in early attachments may permeate into ongoing adult relationships with the specific people involved (i.e. mothers and fathers) often resulting in a continued source of unpleasantness and distress. Similarly, it seems that these ongoing relationships can be mirrored in an LE persistence in trying to stay connected to their LO in some way following rejection, often becoming a source for resultant unease, shame, and humiliation.

Along with these factors, Baumeister & Wotman (1992) note that issues of damaged self-esteem can be central to *would-be lover* [LE] experiences involving rejection. However, in the limerence trajectory, they are particularly significant given that self-esteem may often be implicated in the predisposition to limerence, so that a rejecting blow will be particularly hard. Even in cases where self-esteem had been high at the start, rejection can have a significant impact. For example, *"I think one of my problems [with having been rejected] is that it has shaken my world view. I don't trust my feelings anymore. I was a confident, happy, and loving person. Now I think I must have become revolting." (Undisclosed Author).* Additionally, the blow to self-esteem can be made more devastating by the paradox that *rejecters* [LO] often attempt to delay the rejection as part of the *conspiracy of silence*, which simply serves to make the event more damaging when it finally comes to the *would-be lover* [LE] (Baumeister & Wotman, 1992).

Interestingly, self-esteem is also relevant to the *rejecters* [LO] role since while some have their self-esteem boosted (at least temporarily) if they realise they are being idealised; similarly, it is acknowledged that to be liked by someone rated as less attractive and desirable may also have the unfortunate opposite effect of deflating self-esteem and associated egos. Lastly, it is worth noting that it is self-esteem that is also relevant whenever a limerence experience is played out or made public in some way. In this case, the *would-be lover* [LE] might regard issues of self-esteem, humiliation, and shame that are key features, as opposed to the *rejecter* [LO] for which issues of self-esteem, guilt, anger, and aggravation are more often discussed. Moreover, while self-esteem issues may be a predisposition toward limerence and/or are the significant factor to suffer primarily within it, they can also become pivotal to recovery following rejection, in that eventually a LE may recognise there is no point diminishing self-esteem further in false hope during a period of limerent *starvation,* with many subsequently wishing the realization and associated action to end the limerent episode could have come sooner.

Unpleasant and painful as rejection is for all parties involved, what it usefully can do is shift the *would-be lover* [LE] to a new script, from aspiring lover to disappointed victim, thus moving the limerent episode along. When there is no clear rejection, the decision of the appropriate time for the LE to shift scripts can become particularly difficult, such that some LE describe longing for rejection to at least end the state of limbo that is in effect—*starvation*.

Starvation
Starvation relates to an accumulation of experiences in which the LE can find no reciprocation, thus diminishing hope, often being a very painful and slow process in the

limerence experience (Tennov, 1999; 2005). While this may occur following a disclosure and/or explicit rejection, it can also occur where neither have been involved. Starvation often relates to the key factors of the *conspiracy of silence.* That being the LO's reluctance to hurt the LE in open rejection, together with the expectation that unwanted attention should cease given the knowledge that they themselves are in no way encouraging attention and thus to persist with hope is futile (Baumeister & Wotman, 1992). Starvation can also occur where the LE's concealment of their feelings has been so effective that the LO remains unaware that any interest is bestowed onto them. Whatever the exact scenario, varied cases of starvation exist in which the LE persists in hope, albeit minimal. To this end, Tennov (1999) notes that for LE "Limerence can live a long time sustained on crumbs" (p104).

Baumeister & Wotman (1992) describe the role of hope and longing as "subjective oscillation" (p160) shifting the script from aspiring hopeful lover to broken heart victim again in a form of self-deception, such that some LO feel forced to be ever more cruel to discourage unwanted attention from their LE. Unfortunately, there are examples of perceived unkind behaviours that LO do to the LE, both unconsciously and consciously, deservedly or not. For example, LE describe how their LO will actively ignore them, or be impolite during conversation such as giving minimal word responses to questions, the use of conversational put-downs or derogatory comments, or even walking away. For example, *"I don't know how many times I have had to finish my sentence to the back of my LO's head!" (Undisclosed Author).*

It is following rejection or during starvation that often LE describe feelings of having been encouraged or lead on by their LO, such that the theme of *blaming* becomes prevalent. Interestingly, Baumeister & Wotman (1992) describe how in comparison, *rejecters* [LO] are motivated to avoid any feelings of guilt and blame so they often deny or downplay any involvement that they may have had in the limerent episode. They note that *rejecters* [LO] are motivated by the need to justify themselves because they have been made morally vulnerable through hurting someone. That is for *rejecters* [LO] the moral conflict regarding moral honesty, which has then hurt someone. To this end, they have committed "guilt without misdeed" (Baumeister & Wotman, 1992. p115) with their best subsequent role being to play *blameless victim*. There is likely to be a stronger feeling of moral obligation or conflict, when *rejecters* [LO] recognise that they did show an initial interest and/or when affection has been encouraged or minimal attempts were made to prevent or dissuade the LE. Certainly, LE suggest that while some LO may not have done the former (i.e. show initial interest) many did the latter (i.e. failed to discourage, etc.), presumably because some LO were genuinely ambivalent and others were interested or merely relented under pressure.

Somewhere along the trajectory following rejection or during starvation, some LE start to feel and sometimes direct anger toward their LO, being particularly notable when they have bottomed out in terms of a self-esteem failure and are beginning the process of rebuilding self-esteem. Indeed, Fisher (2004) describes a frustration-aggression hypothesis, whereby anger is directed at loved ones as part of an abandonment stage, a process that may be unpleasant but is also healthy since the feeling may play a part in extricating the self [LE] from unsuitable or unobtainable matches in order that they can begin to look elsewhere. At this stage, any perceivable unkind actions from the LO toward the LE might be useful, certainly there are accounts where LE describe how their LO had appeared to look upon them with contempt or pity and demonstrate a general moral superiority such that might boil anyone's blood.

Lastly, it must also be added, in defence of any LO, that LE themselves do not always follow exemplary social behaviour. Indeed, Tennov (1999) notes how some have tried all manner of tricks to allure their LO, including suicide attempts or other excitement to provoke interest. However, while many limerent episodes seem to involve the unfortunate experiences of rejection and/or starvation, there are some for which the emphasis is very different such as in the case of minimal attention and/or indeed full reciprocation.

<u>Minimal Attention</u>
Tennov (2005) notes how even minimal attention can sustain the limerent process for some time. In association with this, some LE remark how they notice an element of *cat and mouse games* in their interactions with their LO. That is that there appears to be a process taking place (unconsciously or not)

whereby when LE show greater interest in interacting with their LO, their LO appears to pull away or show less interest such that the LE then pulls away and shows less interest themselves, only to find that the LO responds by reactivating their own displayed interest. These apparently cyclic processes are commonly described and appear to be significant in prolonging the limerent episode. For some LE, even where rejection or starvation has been the theme somewhere along the line, some LO muddied the water by developing a slight infatuation or just forgiveness for the LE, which changes their pattern of behaviour. LO may be inclined to do this, particularly if they perceive the need to recover their ego by having initially evaluated the LE as a less worthy partner. In these cases, LO may at some point, be inclined to reevaluate the LE as more attractive potentially resulting in further confusion and mixed messages.

Thus, why such *push and pull* processes occur may relate to the LO having at least some degree of genuine interest in the LE, or alternatively may simply reflect the fact that a LO has come to enjoy the interest they feel and notice the loss of adoration such that they seek (unconsciously or not) to renew the experience. A more severe and destructive pattern of this process has come to be termed *gaslighting* (Calef & Weinshel, 1981), whereby LE describe how their LO has given attention and then subsequently denied events or reinvented events, aiming to persuade the LE that what was reality is in fact them being deluded. Clearly, this is a particularly unpleasant process for the LE, so to this end it must be worth noting that minimal attention may not always be akin to good attention. Similarly and unfortunately, some LO are *game players*, a classic game in the limerent experience being *Rapo*, whereby early stages including luring another to pursue, taking an ego boost from it, only to then dismiss the target [LE]. Level 1 results in the target [LE] being politely dismissed having elicited interest (You're nice but…). Level 2 results in the target [LE] being dismissed and shamed (Buzz off buster!). Level 3 ends in the target [LE] being lured into physical contact, then being accused of assault (Berne, 2010).

These negative processes are very common in limerence and may in part reflect the fact, as it has already been noted, that becoming an LO can inflate self-esteem and egos, but similarly when attention is undesired, it can also deflate self-esteem and egos. Under the latter circumstances, the likely interactions between LE and LO may become increasingly unpleasant. For example, in addition to *gaslighting* or *game paying*, some LE describe how their LO appears to have a need for them in regard to their borderline personalities or narcissist tendencies, with some describing how their LO used them as a target for when they are hurt or angry. To this extent, it is useful in the limerence experience for LE to consider in what ways they may fulfill some sort of role for their LO (if at all), be it positive or negative or both. In terms of more positive examples, some LE describe their LO as using them as a mentor, rescuer, or simply someone in whom there can be love for free. Overall, consideration of these issues might help add some clarity to what the relationship (if there is one at all) is really about and whether, even if it were to develop toward full reciprocation, it would be a relationship that is truly healthy and desired by one or either parties.

Full Reciprocation or Consummation

In terms of full reciprocation, it will apparently depend on what the particular circumstances are (such as whether either party has a SO or is married) as to whether the event provides total bliss or is in fact tempered by the likely path into stormy water. Presumably, bliss pertains most readily when both parties are available for a relationship such that they can set off together (at least for a while). Certainly, full reciprocation does happen, and there are examples of LE who have enjoyed long relationships with an original LO. However, in these cases, while a lasting attachment may have occurred, coexisting serial limerent episodes may also play out. Indeed, some LE give examples of subsequent limerent episodes interrupting their long-term relationships. For the most part, such LE opt actively to conceal their feelings for a new LO, and as such, estimates of the numbers involved would be particularly difficult to identify.

Notwithstanding full reciprocation, there are those LE who engage in consummation as part of/or as distinct from full reciprocation, occurring both regularly or occasionally, pleasurably or not. That is, it is noteworthy that while many an LE would apparently dream of and indeed some report the bliss that consummation can bring, there are also those who report the actual experience to be a significant letdown. It seems it may be difficult for reality to live up to the wonders of fantasy created in the mind when it comes to actually having sex with an LO.

Tennov (2005) described consummation as an expression of intention to enter into a long-term sexual relationship, rather than sex per se. To this extent, it may be useful for LE to have put some thought into exactly what type of relationship they would want their LO to be part of, from long-term committed to intimate encounter only (Gorski, 1993). However, it is amazing how LE apparently find themselves confronted with full reciprocation or consummation, only to realise they do not want an actual relationship or they have no clear plan about where they really would like the relationship with their LO to go! The other key factor here for those LE who, as it turns out had no relationship plans after all, is whether either full reciprocation or consummation can actually end the limerence episode? On this interesting point, it seems that LE who do actually conduct varied relationships with their LO concur that the limerence subsided. But such LE may still acknowledge feelings of being out of control, with idealization and obsessions regarding their LO, which sustained into the longer term.

Transference
An alternative strategy for ending a limerent experience is by utilizing transference (Tennov, 2005). Unfortunately, though, this process merely simultaneously starts another limerent episode, albeit with a new LO! Obviously, transference may be a good idea when the current limerent episode is particularly unpleasant or disturbing, particularly if the new LO

might be a healthier target (such as someone who will better enjoy the attention or may hopefully even reciprocate). Additionally, transference often involves a boost (albeit temporary) to self-esteem, which may have been in decline for some time. However, that said, limerence, whether it is transferred or not, represents a situation far from ideal. Indeed, mostly LE would describe transference as a mere *delay strategy,* recommending instead that at some point consideration for the root cause of limerence will need to be found. Moreover, LE note that given the uncontrollable aspects of the limerence experience it is almost impossible to force transference, much as it may be required or desired.

Friendship
Baumeister & Wotman (1992) have said that often it is within friendships that a path can be lead to unreciprocated love, and in such cases, it is often when self-esteem may suffer worst of all, since the *rejecter* [LO] is likely to have known the *would-be lover* [LE] longer and more intimately, thus making rejection directly personal. Certainly, there are LE who report falling into limerence within preexisting friendships, and of these situations, one of the key themes becomes about their ability to manage the limerence successfully, so that each interaction is not needy and painful. Such LE also describe how often limerence within friendships makes the question of whether to disclose feelings or not particularly pertinent, since to disclose may achieve reciprocation or at least an explanation for awkward or unusual limerent behaviours, but more likely may just bring additional

awkwardness and complications. It seems that the contradiction for these LE is that friendship without honesty (i.e. disclosure) is not a real friendship at all. Similarly, LE recognise that in friendship there should be a role for genuine care toward the LO, rather than an overriding impetus for emotional reciprocation at any cost, with the latter paramount to the limerent experience.

Another key theme for LE is whether those that were not originally friends with their LO can *become* friends? To this question, the answer seems to be both yes and no. That is, yes (if your LO will allow you to be friends), but unfortunately, it is likely that *being friends* will merely prolong limerent suffering. Having said that there are accounts whereby becoming friends with a LO has apparently helped the limerence fade, a process some regard as *immersion*—that is, getting to know a LO better often reduces the ability to idealise them. For example, *"I had thought it would be best if my LO left, but actually, I can see it might be okay. Occasionally, I notice something she says or does which I don't like and that is all helping toward making her human and less goddess."* (Undisclosed Author).

Overall, it seems that being friends with an LO, be it either a preexisting or new friendship, is possible but most successful for those LE who have achieved some sort of acceptance that their limerence will not result in emotional reciprocation. Additionally, these LE also often describe an ability to tolerate access to their LO in close proximity and still cope with the common unpleasant attributes of the limerent experience, such as jealousy. Sadly, sometimes either the LE or the LO (or both) feel that they have to end, or not enter into friendships, because the effects of limerence are too painful to be allowed to play out.

Irrespective of whether an LE has already been rejected, or rejection is pending giving closure to the *conspiracy of silence,* whether they are currently in starvation or undergoing the sometimes tricky process of transference attempts, and even those in varied states of so called friendships – the way forward may be best achieved by beginning a process of *hard inner work*. Such work will need to involve understanding who the LO *really is* and what they have *become* to the LE. Those (many might want to call lucky) LE who have actually elicited full reciprocation or consummation from their LO, will most likely have had this sort of inner work forced upon them as they seek to accommodate and assimilate their LO into their real lives. Eventually, most LE come to the recognition that the integration of the limerent experience is likely to require less LO-orientated rumination and more rational self-oriented thinking.

Chapter 3

Practical Strategies Part 1: Replacing Addictive Ruminative Thinking With Rational Thinking

The limerent experience involves two distinct and interrelated factors: the *imagined* LO (the LO as it appears in the LE mind) vs the *real* LO (the real life LO). While the *imagined* LO may share similarities with the *real* LO, the former often includes idealization and fantasy, which the latter is unlikely or may struggle to live up to in reality. Both are implicated in the LE tendency to contemplate *signs,* particularly those relating to potential emotional reciprocation, with *signs* being a part of obsessive thinking and rumination common to the limerence experience. Ultimately, differentiating between the *imagined* and *real* LO, breaking the habit of rumination and obsessive thinking and refocusing thinking from the LO to the LE *Self* are all key strategies toward recovery in the limerent episode.

<u>Signs</u>
One of the key themes LE discuss with regard to their *real* LO is how every interaction with them is followed by considerable contemplation as regard to whether there were any *signs* for hope of emotional reciprocation. These *signs* may be positive to negative

on an associated continuum of euphoria to despair, with LE describing how they use such *signs* as a *launch pad for their emotions* with states persisting until the next opportunity to interact with their LO.

Interpreting the *signs* may involve conversations being replayed, body language reviewed, and electronic messages reread endless times. Indeed, *signs* may take on their own life whereby scenarios are created and tested out by the LE. For example, Tennov (1999) described a case study of how a particular LE would decide that if their LO chooses to sit in a particular chair close to them at a forthcoming meeting, that would be a positive *sign*. Indeed, some *signs* may make good sense as cues toward attraction, such as whether an LO might try to sit close by, but some are so diverse and unlikely such that any LO (reciprocating, willing or not) might fail to get it right.

Often LE are aware that their pursuit of *signs* is often tenuous. But often times, they are impeded by the fact that they have not disclosed their limerent experience to anyone else so there is no opportunity to receive an objective view of (1) what a useful and appropriate *sign* of emotional reciprocation might be in the first place and (2) whether there is any actual evidence of it in relation to the LO toward the LE. At this point, LE berate their *limbicbrain* for making it almost impossible for them to make an accurate judgment of the situation during interactions, let alone assessing what (if any) associated feelings the LO may experiencing.

Certainly, LE recognise in retrospect a significant number of behaviours, sentiments, and even personality traits that they have wrongly ascribed to the LO (again, be them positive or negative). For those LE who would admit to finding it difficult to recognise any positive *signs* from their LO (i.e. such as those in *starvation*), they still possess all sorts of alternative delaying strategies to avoid the often inevitable fact that the LO is *not interested*. Such elaborate examples as to why their LO has not shown a positive *sign* include those relating to how *busy* or *forgetful* they are, right through to the absolute classic theme of *my LO is shy*.

Whenever an LE describes their LO as "shy", a red warning light should alight, such to pervade even the *limbicbrain,* since often this is not a good scenario. Now obviously, some LO are shy, but more often, shy is in fact *not interested* but currently under the *conspiracy of silence* (Baumeister & Wotman, 1992), such that the LO hasn't yet been able to reject or indeed some *shy* LO simply haven't even noticed the LE (such is the art of the LE concealment). In order to attempt to differentiate between the genuinely *shy* LO and the *not interested* LO, in retrospect LE often realise that their perceptions of shy included, for example, if their LO blushed, looked down at their feet, or generally failed to make eye contact during interactions, with such gestures subsequently being better identified as *embarrassment*. That is often embarrassment for and on behalf of the LE for the error that they are persistently making in being *overfriendly*. In such cases, LE have come to realise that the shyness they encounter from their LO does not in fact extend to how their LO interacts with their own friends or anyone else for that matter. Ultimately, LE have cited then that if a LO is *shy*, this may be a *sign* of *noninterest,* which is ignored through the overwhelming influence of hope and uncertainty in the limerent experience. However, their warning would be that even the shy *starve* and/or *reject* in the end.

In terms of progress from the limerent episode then, there is eventually a need to reevaluate the experience in reflection, and sometimes, this involves recognizing reality-based events were not the *signs* that had been previously thought. For example, *"I can see now what an idiot I have been and how unreciprocated the situation really was. My LO continues to be around and in fact has been chatting to me more than ever recently. There was a time I would have jumped for joy with that sign, but now I know that it probably reflects that she likes me…. that is to say (1) I'm pleasant, (2) I'm always interested in what she says, (3) I laugh at her jokes etc. That's it, that's all there ever was to it!"* (Undisclosed Author).

Interestingly, LE not only concern themselves with *signs* that they perceive from their LO but they are also fixated on the *signs* that they themselves may (intentionally or not) give way. Such that LE fall into the contradiction that they hope for emotional reciprocation from their LO, while simultaneously acting to conceal their own *signs* of attraction, including being overwhelmed, excited, happy, overfriendly, flirty, too agreeable, laughing too much at LO jokes, responding too soon to messages, being too interested and available - through to being shy, stuck for words, awkward, unable to make eye contact, not standing up for oneself in confrontation, being grumpy, nervous, or even frightened. Again in retrospect, when LE eventually met with a more reality-focused living they may be pleased that they attempted to conceal their own *signs*.

Real LO

In order to try and separate the *imagined* vs the *real* LO (i.e. the person who exists in reality without idealization), it is useful to emphasise that the latter is likely to involve a mixture of good and not so good attributes on account of being human, and as such, it can be useful to write a list of their "faults, failings, and imperfections" (Tennov, 1999. p259). Even though Baumeister & Wotman (1992) note that actions such as these are in fact difficult tasks to undertake with derogation often being unconvincing; it definitely is a task that LE do attempt at times. Thus, LE might suggest that their *real* LO can have numerous personal, behavioural, or life circumstances failings such as—too much or too little facial hair, messy haired, or overly made up (separate the male from female LO as you will), generally unhealthy such as smoking, taking drugs, or not getting enough exercise, over interested in specific subjects such as sport or music, no dress sense, generally late, broke, or having a SO or spouse, etc.

Additionally, LE often confer about the relative states and traits that they believe are associated with their LO, and to this end, it is useful to be mindful that, just as there are many underlying and coexisting attributes that may be relevant to the LE, there is likely to be some or others that the LO possess such as: emotional immaturity and lability, being insincere, disrespectful, manipulative, unreliable, mysterious, or being an egoist with multiple admirers. Indeed, whatever the personal attributes of the LO are, under the influence of LE adoration (made explicit or with concealment attempts), even the least likely LO might succumb toward some common issues such as narcissism or codependency. Clearly, since this is an interactional relationship, it is very difficult to assess any accurate states or traits pertaining to the LO, and certainly, the LE *limbicbrain* is not a reliable tool to use for such purposes. But it must be the case that of the many different LO, some may have a range of difficulties such as anxiety and depression or communication difficulties, such as Asperger's Syndrome, and if so, no wonder that the limerent experience often involves a trajectory of mixed messages and confusion.

Where limerence is reciprocated in some way by the *real* LO, attempts to tolerate any negative attributes, states, and traits becomes necessary, as does the impetus to achieve some sort of integration of the *imagined* vs *real* LO if the relationship is to best flourish. Indeed, some LE report struggling with the problem of attempts at integration for some time, others give up and acknowledge that they persist in an unrealistic *imagined* LO idealization and fantasy, which they then try not to act out for the sake of the ensuing confusion that it can cause. Moreover, some LE find that they eventually have to end the longed-for relationship when the incongruity between the *imagined* vs *real* LO remain too uncomfortable to be tolerated.

Another significant factor regarding the *real* LO is that they can oftentimes (perhaps unwittingly) become screens the LE can project fantasies onto. Eigen (2005) describes the issues of projection based on the theory of Carl Jung in an article titled *Is it Love or Is it Projection*. The article recounts how Jung suggested that there is a phenomenon of projecting our *anima* or *animus* (being contra-sexual self-images in the unconscious) on to each other. As a sense of *wholeness* is sought, projection occurs (inevitably since there is no other way to see them), and these images are brought to the open. Intoxication and intensity are cues that projection has occurred. With women, an *animus* or idealised masculine can be projected, and for men, an *anima* or inner feminine is projected based on a collective unconscious composed of parents, siblings, teachers, etc. By taking back projection, it is possible to value the target [LO] for whom they really are, "for as long as we are seeking to be completed by another person, we will not allow them their own autonomy".

So it is then — that the *real* LO has less to do with limerence, as compared to the *imagined* LO, and almost nothing to do with recovery.

Imagined LO

Obsessive thinking and vivid imagery, especially of reciprocation, are a particular feature of limerence during intense periods (Tennov, 1999). When LE describe how they constantly think about their LO, it may well include endlessly repeating interactions with the LO in order to interpret any *signs* of potential emotional reciprocation, including replaying conversations, but also might include conducting imaginary conversations. The latter may be pure fantasy or have a basis in some sort of reality (i.e. something an LO has actually said or done). Alternatively, they may occur as a result of an event in the LE's day unrelated to the LO (Tennov, 1999). For example, it can be the case that an LE is out shopping and finds themselves needing to choose between products, with this thought immediately involving the consideration of which product the LO might prefer to select. Such a process (time allowing) can develop into more intricate and complicated fantasy involving the LO, and as such, then the *imagined* LO is born.

For LE, the *imagined* LO takes on a life of its own, it is always available and can be as agreeable or disagreeable as required. Any number of scenarios can be acted out. They are often multiple and wide ranging (from arguing to making love/ or social to personal), sometimes, but not always, including a theme of the longed-for emotional reciprocation. Interestingly, Tennov (1999) suggested that in limerent fantasy, women tended to link sex and love more readily than men, but whether this finding still holds is yet to be discerned. Certainly, what does seem to occur, irrespective of the attributes of the LE is that the *imagined* LO comes to affect whole identities. Indeed at the height of limerence, LE report how they start to think about their LO as soon as they wake, through until last thing before they go to sleep. Often a significant theme for LE is how they dream about their LO, or that is to say their LO features in their dreams.

In terms of dreams in limerence, just as they are during other life events, some appear quite literal in meaning and easy to interpret. Whereas others are apparently more complicated and confused, especially those that leave the LE trying to decipher what symbolic meaning they may have involved. Dream themes in limerence sometimes mimic the real situation of the LE. For example, some are trying to talk to their LO but find them to be evasive or some appear to involve the LO in pure fantasy. Often, LE describe a sense of unease or anxiety in their limerent dreams, which carries over to their waking. Some LE experience nightmares, and interestingly, some describe the occurrence of repeating dreams, with one area where dreams appear to become a particular torment during separation from the LO (forced or self-induced). Premonition or prophetic dreams are also common, and of course, there are incidences of pleasurable dreams, which all add to the sense of perceived connection to the LO. Thus it is that dreams, whatever their type, content, duration, or frequency, often become a further source (as if another were needed!) of *signs* to be interpreted.

Having an *imagined* LO, whether it is expressed consciously such as in actively thinking about or unconsciously such as in dreams, may be akin to childhood experiences of imaginary friends or companions (Taylor, 1999; Taylor, Carlson, Maring, Gerow & Charley, 2004). The function of imaginary companions being largely for entertainment and enjoyment, however Taylor & Mannering (2007) note how such companions are often said to resemble characters in novels, in that they can take on their own lives especially in terms of being argumentative or critical! Notably, such companions in children can also deflect blame, vent anger, convey information indirectly, with Taylor (1999) stating "Imaginary companions love you when you feel rejected by others, listen when you need to talk to someone, and can be trusted not to repeat what you say" (p63). These sentiments might easily be transposed to the experience of LE with their *imagined* LO, certainly LE recognise them as a fictional character that can be used in a safe place for role playing, *companionship,* or as a form of *escapism*. In this sense, LE are also aware that the *imagined* LO is often used as a strategy (unconsciously or not) to fill a *void,* sense of *emptiness* or *disassociation* commonly reported.

One of the critical factors for the LE about the invention and development of the *imagined* LO regards the association with rumination. The term rumination refers to a process similar to worry whereby there is often excessive thinking that can be marked by intrusive thoughts, followed by avoidance thoughts, which when applied to health-related events are said to involve individuals *dosing* themselves with tolerable and diminishing levels of intrusive thought over time (Horowitz & Kaltreider, 1980). In health rumination, some argue that it is both the frequency and intensity of thoughts that can diminish over time (Janoff-Bulman, 1992; Lepore, 1997). As applied to limerence, LE appear to describe a similar process whereby LO rumination may involve excessive thinking about the *signs*, fantasizing, or daydreaming, which is then interrupted by conscious attempts toward avoidance thinking with the interplay of both gradually diminishing over time, or more specifically, the success rate of avoidance thoughts becoming more noted thus providing positive feedback. For example, some LE describe attempts to limit rumination to specific times, or that is to consciously enable intrusion and then practice avoidance for ever longer periods. Fisher (2004) makes some useful suggestions for avoidance techniques as being to forcibly switch to thinking about [LO] faults, or to transfer the rumination into the subject of someone or something else instead. Most importantly, notwithstanding the prolific role for rumination in limerence, there does at least appear to be an ability to ground rumination in some sort of reality, that is to say, luckily even at the limerence heights, it is possible (to some degree at least) to temper (or at least not act out) any totally delusional intrusive thoughts.

However, what does seem to be particularly ominous about rumination is that it is often habit forming. Habit loops can be useful timesavers, with a biological basis in the basal ganglia in the brain. However, they can also be destructive, involving neurological cravings with cues and rewards. Usefully, Duhigg (2012) describes how while habits can emerge without permission, they can also be changed successfully such as in the case of the undesired behaviours of alcoholism or unhealthy snacking and, as such, may also be modifiable in limerence. Thus, even when the LO has become a source of longing or craving, a new habit can be created by keeping old cues and delivering old rewards but with a different routine. For example, rather than using interactions with the LO as a way of obtaining a feeling of well-being, when noticing the cue of feeling low, LE can create their own high, having replaced LO interaction with an alternative routine such as brief exercise or positive self-affirmation task instead, *et voila* new habit. Clearly, this is simplistic, and Duhigg (2012) himself recognises that, with habits, it is not necessarily easy to modify them and many factors may be relevant. In particular is the fact that individuals do best when they utilise implementation intentions or plans (Gollwizer, 1999). Additionally, there is a need to believe that it is feasible to change, and to this extent, Duhigg (2012) recommends incorporating a community of others (be it even one other person) offering support.

Given the recognised advantage of support, it is particularly sad that LE are often isolated in their limerent journey, and even those that do have some sort of support, report a reluctance to change. Indeed, LE frequently describe that even contemplating steps to distancing themselves (mentally or literally) from their LO is akin to grief. This feeling is in association with a *sense of longing* that often LE describe, such that to step away from either the *imagined* or *real* LO would be *as if* they are dead and, as such, a very difficult and painful process indeed. Those LE that do attempt to step away often recount definite symptoms associated with the classic stages of grief being—denial, anger, bargaining, depression, and acceptance (Kubler-Ross & Kessler, 2005). This may be particularly apparent and abrupt for LE that face rejection since Baumeister &

Wotman (1992) note that *"would-be lover* [LE] faces a brutal and painful process of adjusting to deprivation and learning to stop needing something around which his life has revolved" (p3). Furthermore, given the *grief-like* states that LE often describe, the apparent need to simultaneously regain old pleasures or create new ones seems particularly difficult. However, grief is a process, apparently, and as such, somewhere along the way all things may be possible.

Surprisingly perhaps, often the development of the *imagined* LO is insidious such that the LE is not fully aware of the pervasive effects caused. Certainly, some LE are surprised, when they start to set about a process of recovery, to learn that there are in fact *two* LO that they need to address (the *imagined* vs the *real),* and unfortunately, both can be addictive and both may need to be grieved for in the end. Whatever the processes needed to achieve recovery in the limerent experience, a clear starting point is the necessity to stop and take a moment to compare and contrast the *imagined* vs *real* LO, with the aim of gaining insight and eventually facilitating a perhaps necessary *divide and conquer* approach.

As long as there is uncertainty and hope, there will be *signs* to be endlessly reviewed and self-managed. LE suggest the key is in recognizing this pattern and accepting that it exists. Some describe letting the process wash over them as if they are observers of their own practices, and allowing, for the first time, often a small space for an alternative activity to occur. One that has been overlooked, and one that is surely long overdue. That is, rather than focus on varied and multiple cues, there has been a switch of thinking about the LO primarily, to thinking about the *Self*. Sooner or later, LE seem to come to recognise that they need to find the space and place to think mostly about themselves and their own processes as a move toward rational reality-centered living. From this place of insight, they can move on to thinking about the specific addictive and compulsive behaviours that are associated with their limerence episode with a view to making necessary and positive changes.

Chapter 4

Practical Strategies Part 2: Interrupting Addictive & Compulsive Behaviours

In association with addictive and compulsive thinking, LE describe how they also struggle with inappropriate and uncontrolled behaviours regarding their LO. For example, LE describe how they could go to extraordinary lengths to look better and present themselves in a more positive light to their LO. These behaviours are often associated with the feeling of longing, but are also particularly evident when there are occasions for actual interactions with their LO. Indeed, during actual interactions with their LO, a further set of problematic behaviours can be most evident, those relating to the physiological symptoms of limerence. At some point, when LE start to consider and attempt a change to their addictive and compulsive behaviours, the following themes emerge—a recognition that there are *boundary* issues to be addressed, the potential need to eventually attempt *No Contact* (NC), or at least *Limited Contact* (LC), and lastly, the difficult decision as to whether to *disclose* (i.e. share their limerent feelings) and to whom.

<u>Boundary Issues</u>
Boundaries, whether they are consciously observed or not, are normally accepted behaviours that differ

between people dependent on their perceived interrelationships. Interpersonal boundary issues include those related to actual interaction such as nonverbal (e.g. personal distances and touching), and verbal communication (e.g. conversation and expression of emotion), as well as remote communication (e.g. email or text) and, in LE case, may also include stalking behaviours. Boundaries are present in how people behave toward others and how people allow others to behave toward them (in as far as they can control others behaviour that is!). For LE, unlike most other relationships in their lives, the relationship with their LO is often described as having a number of boundary issues. Additionally, along with being aware of the apparent muddle or blurring of boundaries between themselves and their LO, LE may also be aware of the forms of pleasure that pushing boundaries can bring. But ultimately, LE often subsequently become aware that such actions may be uncomfortable for one or all involved to varying degrees.

In terms of boundaries regarding nonverbal communication, such as personal distance and touching, some LE describe how they long to be close to or touch their LO. Indeed, the idea of their LO reaching out and touching them is highly sought and desired, probably given the link to gestures of longed for emotional reciprocation. LE may already recognise that they stand in too close proximity, or make attempts to touch their LO in ways that might be considered preliminary for flirting (e.g. brushing against them, patting their arm). This behaviour from LE may sometimes occur as a result of the clumsiness and awkwardness during an interaction or other times has been more planned and rehearsed. The motives for such behaviour include pushing the boundary to gauge the response from a LO, often resulting in the LO sending back mixed messages as they might initially be flattered or, if not flattered, then increasingly confused. Indeed, it seems some LO engage in unconsciously mirroring back or some purposefully encourage such behaviours, with both such actions from the LO resulting in a further blurring of boundaries, at least for a while.

For LE who do get the opportunity to converse with their LO, (that is those who are in a position to and physiologically able to, i.e. not speechless), some describe how they have boundary issues regarding inappropriately personal, frequent, or lengthy conversations. Often such conversations are also unusual in their content in terms of including disproportionate regard for topics relative to any SO or spouses or in that they completely omit mention of any such relevant people. Problems regarding communication also extend to electronic mail, whereby there may often be additional issues, such as when LE describe how they are forever longing and waiting for electronic messages from their LO, with unfortunate incidences where text are sent in error etc., probably reflecting the tendency of the LE to frequently select and review their LO contact details and messages. For those LE for whom messages do arrive from their LO, the result often involves the LE berating themselves for replying too soon, inappropriately, and with too long a response.

A further facet of conversation whereby boundary issues may exist between LE and LO is the role of emotional expression. LE notice how they regularly have to control their urge to express their feelings toward their LO, but also how emotion in general is more surface and apparent in conversation. Again, this may sometimes result in the LO mirroring back behaviour, albeit consciously or not. Such emotional repertoires may be positive but are also apt to include more negative emotion, especially toward the LE as time unfolds. Ultimately, some LE describe a pattern of increasingly negative interactions whereby the LO comes to more often show their frustration, disregard and disrespect. For the unlucky LE, this may end in an emotional outburst, whereby either the LE overexpresses themselves and/or the LO finally verbalises rejection for the LE.

Boundary issues may also involve behaviours that do not necessarily involve personal interaction, such as in the form of stalking, be it literal or cyber, with such behaviour also extending to friends and family of the LO (albeit to a lesser extent). Some LE describe how they are ashamed to admit the ridiculous acts that they have performed in order to *get a sight of*, *get closer to,* or *impress* their LO. For example, some LE follow their LO, walk past their house, office, or classroom, arrive at the same destinations, or shop at the same stores. They may also note their car number plate, take pictures of and/or even record their LO's voice. Some LE have saved things that their LO has given them or other people, or even saved things that their LO just touched! Presumably, the potential goal of stalking along with simply getting a *fix* for the addiction to LO, is often to find out what the LO might like in order that more information can be sought and later manipulated, or indeed to find out where the LO might be so as to attempt to coincide.

There are, of course, many problems associated with stalking including what to do with any knowledge gained, issues of jealousy, and legal considerations. In regard to any information gathered, there are many limits to what exactly can be purposefully done with such new knowledge. For example, the information found out cannot be used in conversation since the LE hasn't been officially told about it, thus oftentimes such information becomes a burden of things to remember *not to mention* and as such tends to clog up the LE working memory—no wonder actual interactions between LE and LO can be awkward. Worst, where LE possibly *finds out* something they believe their LO might like to know about, there is a risk of sharing the information. But obviously, rarely will such a gesture go well, since LE would have simultaneous exposed themselves as both stalker and meddler.

Together with limitations in terms of the usefulness of stalking, there is also a recognised problem of evoking feelings of jealousy for the LE, or mate guarding as it is sometimes termed (Fisher, 2004). Tennov (1999) recognises the issues of jealousy as related to the need for exclusivity. She notes, in limerence, it is not who is slept with but whether feelings are returned that is paramount. Thus, LE describe how they busily try to work out the interconnections between players around the LO life, (both who they are and how loved they are) often on limited information. In so doing, they note how they are apt to ascribing intimate connections where indeed there may be none. Furthermore, when others' lives are viewed *as if* by a spectator, they often look intrinsically more interesting than they probably actually are. Thus, many a dull LO has been made more exciting than their reality. Nowhere is this issue made more apparent than when considering the role of cyber-stalking particularly, since on the internet, LO (as we are all inclined to do) have the bonus of being able to largely manipulate their image in a form of self-presentation and promotion. As such, it is no wonder that some LE come to overestimate the skills, complexity, and popularity of their LO's lives, making their own look meagre by comparison.

The range of common cyber-stalking sites includes general searches, maps of associated addresses, photo and video sharing sites, online games, and of course, social networking sites, or indeed anywhere else any sort of information about the LO might be. Of these targets, the ones that provoke the most concern are the social networking sites and, to a lesser extent, photo or video sites. These seem particularly problematic since, for those LE connected to their LO, there is the persistent problem that information about their LO is readily available to search and that such information may in fact arrive unprompted onto the LE's own site, even when they themselves are not actively cyber-stalking. This persistent, irregular, and omnipresent aspect of such social networking sites seems to feature in LE's ongoing distress. For LE that are not already connected to their LO, such social networking sites also offer a constant source for pontificating as to whether they should *friend request* them or, later in the limerent experience, whether they should *defriend* them. Indeed, some LE see the process of *defriending* as pivotal to their continued recovery from a limerent episode. For example, *"I have not seen my LO for a while, but I know I was still stalking him on [social network site]. Now I've defriended, and I really believe that it is the best possible thing that I could have done at this time. I have noticed that I am not thinking about him anywhere near as often as I was before" (Undisclosed Author).* Indeed, such *defriending* is often in addition to a range of related strategies whereby the LE attempt to reduce or stop online stalking behaviours, together with deleting all known contact addresses, emails, texts, etc. belonging to their LO.

In addition to the inclination toward a range of stalking behaviours, LE also recognise there is something unusual about the frequency—with some LE describing activity of 5 times or more daily at the height of the episode (particularly regarding cyber-stalking). Clearly, almost anyone might get the urge to stalk another person at some point, to at least a lesser degree and particularly online, but for LE, the urge can be described as overwhelming. Interestingly, it is at this point that such LE appear to recognise that they have lost significant self-control and, in this recognition, act to get varied forms of help and support. Often LE describe how they attempt to stop stalking behaviour but then find they relapse, making them feel especially awful and resolved to try harder next time. Some note a satisfaction from resisting the urge, such that they are aware that they are regaining control. Some describe how they were gradually able to regulate their stalking behaviours to just once a day, then once every few days etc. until they were finally able to stop. Often LE described their fear that their LO or SO or spouse might find out, with such exposure being perceived as exceptionally degrading and humiliating.

Most significantly, LE are aware that stalking can in fact be termed illegal. As such, in particular regard to cyber-stalking, LE anxiously debate to what extent it might be possible for a LO to track such targeted activity. Certainly, increasingly there does appear to be a service industry that is offering web-based traffic tracking to this effect. Indeed, LE describe how the fear of being found out in whatever their particular stalking behaviour might be is often paramount in their attempts to modify what has otherwise been an uncontrollable behaviour. Most importantly, LE note that at no point do they ever intend to harm or distress their LE. Indeed, it is very difficult for LE to think in any way negatively about their LO or to recognise their faults, let alone intend harm or distress. In fact, in a typology of stalkers, it has already been identified that those motivated by versions of love can be a nuisance, but are a low risk for any forms of aggression (Mullen, Pathe & Purcell, 2000).

Recognizing boundary issues, be they interpersonal (e.g. touching or intimate conversation) or remote (e.g. stalking), the tendency becomes more salient as the limerent experience develops. This is in accordance with the unfortunately familiar trajectory whereby the LO becomes increasingly confused and the LE more desperate, combining to create ever more awkward and unpleasant interactions. It seems it is often at this point that the LO is reluctantly forced to define their boundaries more clearly, leaving the LE knocked back or rejected. As this pattern of unfortunate behaviour plays out, these LE complain how their LO treat them badly in their opinion. However, more hopefully, it seems that most LE have also realised that they need to respect boundaries that have been set and further, to find it within themselves to begin the long and difficult process of identifying and setting some long overdue boundaries of their own. To this end, the ultimate boundary setting that LE can perform is to go NC, or at the very least LC.

No Contact

Tennov (1999) was clear "the best cure [for limerence] is No Contact" (p261). Most LE would recommend at least a short period of NC, which means not allowing themselves to see, speak to/hear from their LO in any way. So along with avoiding personal contact, this might also involve no phone calls, text, email, definitely no stalking (be it literal or virtual). In reality then, as Tennov (1999) suggests, LE may need to change their own routines by rescheduling classes, seminars, work meetings, or social gatherings to generally avoid wherever they think their LO might be. They may also need to change the bus ride home, park in a new place, counter any *potential LO drive past* opportunities by choosing an alternative, even if inconvenient and longer route to their destination. In extension, they may also need to avoid LO's friends or their own friends who are likely to mention LO's name. Indeed, some LE go as far as deleting all known contact details, including defriending on social network sites and even changing courses, jobs, home addresses in an attempt to remove LO from their lives.

While the use of NC remains controversial among LE, with some believing any form of distancing merely prevents understanding, there certainly does seem to be consensus from LE, who albeit reluctantly agree that NC, even if for just a short period of say 2-3 weeks or months, is useful. Commonly, LE describe using NC for periods of 4-6 months or more before acknowledging some perceived success and some LE cite years. Importantly, it appears that NC, in allowing the LE to remove the stimulus of the *real* LO, also allows for the growth of a potentially different perspective on the limerent episode and the beginning of a process of taking back personal control. NC can afford a period of clearer reflection on the differences between the *imagined* and *real* LO. Thereafter, with the *real* LO temporarily silenced, NC can be used to deal with the *imagined* LO addiction separately rather than trying to deal with both *imagined* and *real* addictions simultaneously, thus segmenting the limerent episode into two distinct addictive areas with which to overcome. Ultimately, at least one clear advantage that NC may achieve by avoiding the *real* LO is *NO NEW PAIN*. This is often cited as a primary driver toward the need for NC, with LE—particularly in the starvation stage—describing the sadness that they feel following a pattern of recurring negative interactions with their LO, whereby any sign of hope continues to diminish.

In spite of apparent advantages, the decision to attempt NC with an LO is a difficult one, often with many physical and psychological barriers. For example, physically avoiding an LO who has been a close friend, is a friend of the family, a work colleague, or class mate has practical difficulties that may not be easily surmountable. Similarly, LE describe feelings that prevent them taking the NC initiative, which might include statements such as these: *"Though I know I should, I can't accept that the intensity of feeling/connection/soul-mate that I had for my LO was entirely unreciprocated"* or *"If I give it more time, do this, say that, LO might change their mind"* and *"There is such a lot I am learning about myself through this experience of limerence, even though the process is awkward for LO and painful for me" (Undisclosed Author)*. Lastly, LE describe their reluctance or mixed feelings about finally bringing the limerent episode to closure, for example: *"The things I used to like I don't like anymore, I'm lost and without my LO what is my motivation for anything?" (Undisclosed Author)*.

Additionally, it is noted that even those LE who successfully surmount any physical and psychological barriers, thus achieving NC, might well admit that their motives were, unconsciously or not, suspect in that they used NC as just another way (albeit more legitimate way) of being able to focus on their LO. That is, in the case of NC, LE can actively think through and action out ways of avoiding their LO. Alternatively, LE might view

NC as a way of, unconsciously or not, punishing their LO or testing out (and hoping) that their LO might notice their absence and reciprocate in some way. Clearly, these issues are all interesting and valid, but at some point, LE do still make the decision to attempt and stay NC, notwithstanding their reservations or motives, be them conscious or not.

For those LE that do attempt NC, some describe the incidence of how they have broken NC. Often LE break NC because the LO contacts them or because they can no longer cope with abstinence, with such relapses at least serving the purpose of testing out the degree of sensitivity residual toward the LO, with some LE finding contact reverses them immediately back into full limerence and others finding that there has been some desensitization. For those who appear to have broken NC too soon and believe themselves to be back at square one of limerence, the situation can be very disappointing. However, even in these cases, some LE use this negative experience as a new strategy as they attempt NC again. That is, they focus on the desire to avoid further potential feelings of disappointment as a way of sustaining NC next time. This strategy has been termed *anticipated regret* by psychologists and has been successfully used in many health promotion areas (Abraham & Sheeran, 2003).

Other LE do recognise progress following a relapse in NC, albeit minor. Most often, LE appear to acknowledge some degree of setback in limerence symptoms, but note the intensity and duration is diminished. LE often describe how they come to regard every potential occasion for contact that they avoid as a very painful process, but one which offers a sense of victory and a step forward in regaining self-control. Additionally, these lucky LE can begin to recognise then that the limerent experience could, or at least there might be some fragment of hope that it could, actually pass.

Of course, the really lucky LE, who go back into contact with their LO and find that they have none or only few unwanted limerent symptoms, might consider themselves cured. However, it seems that even then they are aware that at best they may always have a warm glow of affection, which is in perpetual danger of relighting, and to that end they may always need to keep any contact brief. Thus, the preferred goal of breaking NC is to realise this progressive step in recovery, whereby contact with the LO no longer triggers a significant unwanted symptom response, allowing the limerent episode to be considered in past tense. That is, the LE is aware of reflection and can describe the limerent episode as something that happened rather than something they are still coping with.

Limited Contact

For those LE for which NC with a LO is simply not a current option, some try a lesser version being: LC. For LE, this may involve a move to not necessarily avoid LO but to no longer actively seek their LO, with any future contact initiated by the LO receiving polite reply only. Alternatively, there may be some attempts to avoid LO but only where feasible and to minimise the duration of contact as much as possible, a practical solution for LE trapped in work related situations for example. Such attempts might be coupled with changing the tone and content of any verbal communication to work subjects only, together with modifying any potential friendlier nonverbal communication.

During LC, LE describe their ongoing struggle to behave more normally in the interactions with LO and their behaviour around their LO generally. Some LE have used distraction techniques, such as holding a stone or precious object in their hand or pocket, which they can squeeze if necessary during interactions with their LO as a way of refocusing back to the *Self* during these awkward or difficult situations. But, by far, the most commonly recommended strategy is called *Fake it till you make it*. For the lucky LE, they may well have experienced a genuine change of heart, which allows them to conduct themselves during interactions with their LO in parity with their own true feelings, but it seems oftentimes there is at least a short period whereby an alternative strategy might best be employed to cope with LC. In *fake it till you make it,* LE describe how they, in spite of any true feelings, change their overt behaviours toward their LO to signify disengagement.

In terms of verbal communication, often LE will have already used strategies such as breathing exercises to calm down before an interaction, preparing a script to help them rehearse their potential lines with LO, and ensuring their voice projects when they do speak to LO. But in LC, they may now also want to: only speak to LO when spoken to, answer in a polite and short style, ask no unnecessary questions and ask no personal questions whatsoever. Similarly, in terms of nonverbal body language, LE describe how they stopped allowing LO to be the focus of attention by acting busy or distracted around them, including talking to other people and excluding the LO, standing to the side of the LO rather than in front of them during any meetings or brief conversations—and DEFINITELY NO EYE CONTACT!

Eye Contact

It seems that for LE, eye contact is high on the list of triggers that sparked the limerence and remains high throughout the limerent experience in whatever shape it takes. Thus LE can recall the first time they looked into their LO's eyes and were aware the look was unusual both in its duration (that is it was slightly longer than the normal 5 seconds intervals) and in its intensity, or that is in the intensity of feeling that was evoked in the LE. Some LE suggest that the conversation they are having with their eyes to their LO appears to, at times, be entirely different from the concurrent verbal conversation. Indeed, LE describe how they may come to look forward to such eye contact with their LO and may indeed then be disappointed on meetings when the longed for eye contact doesn't happen. In this sense then, eye contact in itself appears addictive.

The addictive capacity for eye contact may have scientific grounding since it is recognised that, from infancy, eye gaze provides a number of essential functions such as providing information and regulating interaction, in addition to producing biological markers (e.g. oxytocin), which can induce feelings of well-being

(Moore, 2008; Uvnas-Moberg & Francis, 2003). Later as adults, the biological markers of mutual eye gazing persist, such that in emotional arousal pupil size dilates (Bradley, Miccoli, Escrig & Lang, 2008) and that people perceive eyes to be more shiny or watery, creating a glint or sparkle, thus providing an actual feedback cue for interaction (Morris, 1973). Indeed, any biological foundations of eye gazing have long since been overlaid with a plethora of prose and literature espousing the effects of lovers' eye gazing as soulful connections and often regarding the theme of feeling *at one with* or *becoming whole* during such mutual eye gaze moments.

However, a caveat, while it may be that all this mutual eye gazing and associated emotion is co-occurring, it is also just as likely that only some or indeed none of it might be occurring for an LO and is therefore entirely a reflection of the LE *limbicbrain*. Even for those LO that do not subsequently look away during prolonged eye contact, this may be an indication that they are taking the moment to understand why they are being intensely looked at, or simply not feeling too uncomfortable or even enjoying the feeling of simply being present with another person…indeed, they may even like the LE and be mutually enjoying the moment! We can't really know what another person experiences during such moments of eye contact unless we ask them, and even then, they might lie or they genuinely might not know.

One thing that does appear clearer is that for LE who have experienced rejection from their LO (perceived or otherwise), eye contact can become a nightmare.

"I have never seen eyes so beautiful. It was looking into her eyes where I first fell for her. In her eyes I am suspended into timelessness. There is just her and me, a connection to the soul, and all else disappears. But now to look into her eyes pervades my inner being. In her rejection, I am shattered, I feel resentment and yet I still love, I can't stop loving. I feel shame and embarrassment and now I can see that she is embarrassed for me. So to look into her eyes is to witness my own humiliation. But she cannot possibly understand that I am so far beyond that. I don't think anyone could ever contemplate how totally lost and destroyed I really am ..." (Undisclosed Author).

Whether or not LE concur with the theory that to allow someone to look into their eyes is to risk their soul and other such versions of belief, it does appear that often LE feel that it is very difficult to hide their feelings portrayed through their eyes and to break the spell of their LO if they continue to engage in eye contact or mutual eye gazing with them. Thus eye contact is a key behaviour to consider modifying when interacting with LO during LC. For LE first attempting or working toward LC, those compelled to still look into their LO eyes have at least noted making a different kind of private promise to themselves—that is not to share their feelings verbally.

Disclosing to LO

For LE, to disclose or not to disclose is a significant theme to be pondered and proliferated over. Tennov (1999) suggested that LE should be discouraged from revealing their feelings to others, and indeed, some LE would advocate no disclosure at any cost. That is, at no time will they actually verbally express their true feelings toward their LO, even when directly questioned by their LO or anyone else. This might involve the LE being avoidant or aloof regarding any direct questions or even lying. LE may describe the shame that they feel in terms of having feelings toward their LO and of their overwhelming urge to share them. Such LE might recognise that to disclose would be unnecessary since they have no real purpose of intended relationship with the LO (e.g. they are happily married), and some LE might suggest that to engage in disclosure is just more unnecessary *drama*, risking further humiliation including lost self-dignity, esteem, and respect.

Other LE, at some point, enter into a form of partial disclosure, which may involve dropping hints about their feelings of affection toward their LO and pushing gently at boundaries, such as having increasingly more intimate conversations, with a few brave LE advocating the full disclosure or a radical honesty type of approach (Blanton, 2003). Indeed, the compulsion for LE to tell the LO everything and anything is generally another common theme, with LE describing how they have to regularly withhold the urge to *blurt out* even everyday matters, let alone those regarding the strong feelings and fantasies that they may have about their LO. Some LE describe how they feel that their interactions with their LO have long been conducted in the knowledge that there is *"a gorilla in the room!"*, that is an obvious subject that needs to be talked about but isn't currently being discussed.

Obviously, LE cite a key motive for disclosure as being to discover if the LO reciprocates. But other motives exist, including just wanting to make sense of the experience or change awkwardness in interactions with their LO. For example. *"I am not after emotional reciprocation, but I do want to make some sense of the mad situation that occurred to me and I would also like to deal with the bad karma that is between us" (Undisclosed Author).* Other LE regard simply wanting to bring closure to the limerent symptoms of longing and hope, even if the likely outcome might be rejection. Sometimes LE motivation for disclosure may be to simply cause their LO to become more aware of their actions and thinking.

At the time of disclosure, LE describe an array of feelings partly related to what initial response they get. One hopes, and it presumably occurs at times that there is mutual affection of a type, indeed even mutual limerence. But often LE noted how they got an unclear response, with Baumeister & Wotman (1992) having set out the many reasons for this, including LO difficulty in causing hurt such that they offered a less than truthful or even slightly hopeful response. Some note how disclosure can just make things worse, because even when there is some form of reciprocation, the LE can end up resolving the worry about how their LO feels about them, only to instigate a new worry about how their LO is subsequently going to behave. Sadly, most LE describe how disclosure did not go well. They report how they endured forms of humiliation and excruciating embarrassment, together with feelings of guilt and sadness, and physical symptoms such as feeling tired and sick. This was particularly true, for those LE that found that their LO returned awkwardness, pity, and irritation (especially related to the likely subsequent impairment to friendship or the working relationship).

Unfortunately, the act of full disclosure does often seem to occur at the height of limerent symptoms, sadly at the very point that the LE is least able to assess the situation sensibly and logically, such as to at least partially explain why so many disastrous disclosures do seem to occur. In terms of disclosure (and behaviours in general), a common rule used by some LE is that *"if you notice that there is a clear desire to do something regarding your LO—you likely shouldn't, whereas if you notice that there is a clear desire regarding your LO not to do something—then you likely should!" (Undisclosed Author).* Whatever the immediate outcome of disclosure, some LE later come to regret the event, even though they may have felt it was the right thing to do at the time. For example, *"If I could go back and have the time again, I am basically totally certain that I wouldn't disclose. Okay, it was great to finally get it out there, but it also caused my LO to completely back away and as a consequence I am in desolation. I was incredibly down before I disclosed, but that was nothing compared to the intolerable heartbreak I have now" (Undisclosed Author).*

For a few brave LE, irrespective of the immediate responses that disclosure received, there was also a pattern of relief expressed whereby the deed had been done or the *answer* was finally ousted. However, this theme of potential *self-relief* can be perceived differently for some LE who chose nondisclosure. For these LE, disclosure may be conceptualised as often purely for the self, and in most instances, they would suggest it is in fact too great a burden to off-load built up fantasies onto an LO that could have any range of feelings toward them. Specifically, some LE might suggest that the desire for disclosure may show a lack of regard or respect for the LO, since to disclose would be using the LO for the LE's own personal and spiritual ends.

It could be that whether to disclose or not depends on the LE's and the LO's very particular circumstance. For example, for LE who already knew their LO as a friend, the need for disclosure as some sort of explanation for their limerent behaviour or their need to go LC or NC might be perceived as necessary. Similarly, disclosure might occur for LE who have *become* friends with their LO, that is those who have enjoyed intimate conversation or share social activities together over some time. Thus, LO who were originally friends or who have become friends often fall into the category of those to which LE decide to disclose. Disclosure might also be useful for those who know their LO in work related situations, however here the situation is very delicate since workplace legislation, policy, and procedures become relevant. Whereas for those LE who recognise the relationship they have with their LO is mostly in their head, that is that the *imagined* LO exists more significantly than any reality, disclosure is least likely to be wise. Disclosure might also not be wise where there are genuine barriers, such as where either party have a SO or spouses, such that reciprocation could surmount to undesired affairs or the breakdown of families.

Consideration toward disclosure might usefully also include regard for the LO's perceived personality, this being tricky in itself since limerent idealization tends to overestimate kinder attributes of LO, which may not be objectively evident. Obviously, there are likely to be more negative ramifications of disclosure for those unfortunate LE who have an LO that may be manipulative, egoists, narcissistic, etc. It is sometimes very difficult to be sure exactly what personality attributes a LO might objectively possess and, in fairness, many LE have enabled their LO to become, having spent some time throwing rose petals at them. That said, though, at least some regard toward whether the LO is likely to be a genuinely kind, compassionate, and mature person, whom is willing and capable enough to cope with the knowledge that the LE is wanting to give them, must be prudent to consider predisclosure.

For those LE that do decide on disclosure, be it partial or full, consideration for when and where to do it, as well as aims and tactics, could all be considered useful. Some make the disclosure in person, but others send letters, emails, or text and await the reply. Indeed, there are accounts of unanswered letters and emails to LO, with LE recognizing that no answer is in fact an answer in itself—rejection. Clearly, for LE who require some form of more immediate response, as opposed to potentially none, disclosure is better face-to-face. Alternatively, LE can combine strategies and hand their LO a letter to read in front of them, thus negating the problems of stumbling over words or forgetting part of the disclosure, while ensuring a response from the recipient is guaranteed (well, at the least the LE can watch the LO's response even if they don't verbalise one!). Some LE describe how they used a more social setting for the disclosure event or specifically took along a confident to mediate as required, though others suggested they chose to conduct such a meeting in a more private place, with only their LO present.

Disclosing to the SO or Spouse

Some LE describe how they feel that they *owed it* to their SO or spouse to be honest in telling them the feelings that they are having toward their LO. LE also describe how they needed to disclose because they recognised that they were not successfully keeping their feelings private, rather their feelings were showing in their unusual or distracted behaviour toward the SO or spouse and in their duties toward others. Certainly, LE recognise, particularly in reflection, the guilt and sadness that they felt whereby they *wasted time in limerence land* or neglected their responsibilities toward deserving others such as their children, friends and colleagues (Tennov, 1999).

For LE who are married, there may be the additional complication of the marriage vow, in that there has been some sort of promised fidelity and often married LE describe their feelings toward their spouses of wanting to honor that promise (figuratively and literally). Indeed theorists, such as Shirley Glass (2004) in her book *Not Just Friends,* have described the behaviour of increasing intimacy with others (such as an LO) as entering a double life on a pathway toward emotional and potentially actual affairs. Her recommendation is to build honesty with SO or spouses (such as disclosure), while creating boundaries to others, in order to best rebuild trust and preserve the core relationship.

It seems that in keeping with disclosing to a LO, the act of disclosing to a SO or spouse is also painful and difficult. However again, LE also report feelings of relief, but in this case, it seems the most frequent ramifications are those related to fractured trust, insecurity, and jealousy. Thus, some LE warn against such disclosures, for example, *"For us, the jealousy was too much to live with… my SO left." (Undisclosed Author).* However, for some LE with a SO or spouse, disclosure seemed to bring about positive changes in their relationship too. For example, some LE describe how the experience afforded an opportunity to reorganise their lifestyles and their emotional connections. For example, *"We have been together so long that we were complacent. Mostly, we talked about the kids. But now we are rebuilding trust, spending quality time together, and talking and listening to each other more." (Undisclosed Author).*

Disclosing to Friends & Colleagues
Oftentimes, friends and colleagues had already noted a change in the LE's behaviour (Tennov, 1999), such that when they disclosed about their LO, it was less unexpected than may have been previously thought. Indeed, LE who disclosed about their LO to their friends

and colleagues, mostly described how they benefited from being provided with information, tangible assistance, self-esteem, and companionship support. For example, LE describe how by sharing their experience with a friend, they were introduced for the first time to the online support group communities or related books. In terms of tangible assistance, LE describe incidences such as how work colleagues have helped them to reschedule duties to best avoid the LO, or coworkers taking the LE's place for meetings in order to avoid potentially awkward situations.

Additionally, LE describe how disclosing to friends and colleagues afforded the benefit of self-esteem props and companionship, such as when being offered empathy, a feeling of being valued and a sense of belonging in that the limerent experience is shared by others and that others are still available to the LE for shared activities. LE report how with friends and colleagues they were able to laugh about the countless incidences of ridiculous and awkward interactions that had taken place and how they found out that, though their experiences may be extreme, they are by no means unique. However, it must be noted that not all experiences regarding disclosing to friends and colleagues went well and certainly the negative effects of limerence in the workplace were commonplace, with many in fear of the consequences (Tennov, 1999).

Interestingly, overall, it appears there is significantly more discussion and consideration as to whether to disclose to an LO than to an SO, spouse, friends or colleagues, most likely reflecting the self-oriented aspects of the limerent experience. Indeed, there are accounts of LE noting how they completely forgot that they were already in relationships or giving no regard to friends and colleagues opinions! Even more perversely, some LE acknowledge the role that nondisclosure to other people in their life can afford. It appears that secrecy can become relevant in their limerent experience, in that it becomes a source of arousal and obsession. LE describe how disclosing their secret feelings about their LO can risk dampening these pleasurable effects and thus perpetuate the perceived need for continued nondisclosure toward others.

However, when, in whatever ways, and to whom disclosure happens, LE seem to agree that the preparation and process is incredibly distracting, painful and awkward, but persist presumably in a view that *"the only way out of the abyss is through it" (Undisclosed Author)*. It seems all that LE can do in disclosing is to be as open and honest as is preferred and possible, but also recognise that their target, be it LO, SO, spouse, friends, or colleagues, may simply not want to or not be able to verbalise their own feelings, or that it would have been preferable if they hadn't. Certainly, LE demonstrate respect for other LE that do take the option of disclosure, recognizing the great deal of courage that disclosure takes. Ultimately, in considering whether to disclose or not, prudent LE recommend that its useful to *begin with the consequences in mind*, that is that there is a real need to be clear about why it is being done and what the hopes are for achievement versus the likely scenarios. Ideally,

LE recognise that in any disclosure *"there has to be both trust and respect" (Undisclosed Author).*

In spite of the difficulties, LE do change their addictive and compulsive behaviours, culminating in developing their own boundaries while respecting other peoples. Often LE reduce LO related contact, at least temporarily, and choose whether to disclose or not, according to each LE's circumstances and personal preference. As the limerent trajectory unfolds, LE recognise that they gain insight, but some will take the journey more or less alone whereas others decide to utilise a wider range of support or therapeutic intervention along the way. LE might see neither options as right or wrong, but rather they may suggest that ideally the limerent experience is a journey and, as such, forward is advocated if possible, even if at times there are *a few steps back.* Overall then, LE advocate *one step at a time* toward a *better place*, wherever that place will be.

Chapter 5

Practical Strategies Part 3: Insight & Therapeutic Intervention

Even if you do nothing, time may heal to some or other extent, but for the LE who report unwanted limerent episodes spanning years or even decades sometimes, it seems time is not such a reliable healer. Time may change us, but healing is probably better done proactively. To this extent, there are numerous resources available to LE, from those of the *Self*, including favourites of therapeutic writing and virtual support networks, as well as psychological and pharmaceutical interventions. Throughout, LE describe a key theme of the need to avoid *reescalation* and *reoccurrence* of the limerent episode.

Self as Savior
Often, LE start by looking at self-help books, such as how to cure your addiction to a person (Halpern, 2004), address family problems (Skyner & Cleese, 1993) and mend broken hearts (Rosse, 2001; McKenna & Willbourn, 2006; Webber, 2012). Some LE have expressed their view that reading and collecting these self-help books can become addictive and obsessive in itself! Thus, it is useful to consider the opinion that "self-help books are like car repair manuals: you can read them all day, but doing so doesn't fix a thing.

Working on a car means rolling up your sleeves and getting under the hood, and you have to be willing to get dirt on your hands and grease beneath your fingernails" (Lewis et al, 2001. p177).

The practical applications of self-help knowledge for limerence then seems to suggest key tenets. There is a need to do some *hard inner work*, which broadly speaking often relates to controlling or accepting it. Clearly, there is a place for both, but among LE, there seems to be a clear emphasis in the end toward the latter. Overall, LE concur that at some point there is a necessity to learn to identify and manage thoughts, feelings, and behaviours, including changing any self-defeating core beliefs about *Self*, others, and the world that may have been learned as children (including attachment issues) or as adults. Often, LE come to realise (what mostly they already knew but had set aside) that at some point the need for self-love, self-esteem, forgiveness, compassion, acceptance, and mindfulness become most significant themes.

Huber (2010) suggests that socialization results in the development of many self-hate related voices in our heads or egocentricity (a feeling of being separate from self, others, and life) and recommends that while we can be aware of them, we don't necessarily need to believe them. Socialization teaches that there is *something wrong with us* and that good people are not self-centered, rather than teaching us to love, appreciate, trust, have confidence in, or look to ourselves for guidance. Specifically children develop sub-personalities based on their accumulative experiences that their needs are bad and they are bad for having needs. Perusing perfection follows, but self-hate makes perfection impossible to obtain. She also proposes that it is useful to be mindful of any criticism (constructive or otherwise) from self or others as these are often versions of self-hate. Instead, she advocates learning to live without self-hate, thus resulting in a sense of freedom and spaciousness, loss of identity whereby learning to pay attention and be present in the moment can occur. She states "we are responsible for being the person we have always wanted to find" and "we must learn to give ourselves and receive from ourselves unconditional love and acceptance" (p86).

For LE, there are often examples of the realization that acceptance is a useful strategy to begin to embrace. They describe how they have learned not to enable or reject limerence feelings, but rather to simply become less judgmental and hopefully less anxious and ruminating. In general, LE might concur with the theme of *emotional scanning and awareness* (Zukav & Francis, 2002) and definitely the theme of *watching yourself at work*—that is, watching thoughts and emotions while being *present in the moment* (Tolle, 2001). For example, *"I have been trying to just accept my feelings (especially in LO presence) and just quietly observe them rather than just 1. unconsciously act on them or 2. try to stop or modify them, 'cos the former has just caused more trouble and the latter hasn't worked so far" (Undisclosed Author).* Similarly, learning not to enable or reject limerent bodily sensations is a common theme, with some recognizing sentient experiences of say pain or excitement in the knowledge that they too may be transient. For example, *"In her presence, I feel sadness rise, I can't breathe, my heart sinks, but I just let it happen, I watch it happen, the feelings all swirl around, and after a while, they settle down again." (Undisclosed Author).* Indeed, as in broader literature, some LE go further to add gratitude for any thoughts and feelings, whatever they may be, while others make attempts to dissipate them. For example, *"Sometimes, I imagine my thoughts and feelings in the air and notice that the wind carries them" (Undisclosed Author).* One key point being to recognise, own, and learn from the process (Huber, 2010).

As practical recommendations toward achieving self-love and acceptance more generally, Huber (2010) suggests that you can make a list of things your inner child wants others to say regarding feeling loved and appreciated and then say it to yourself. This list can be taped and listened to daily. She also recommends writing yourself love letters, doing one loving thing for yourself daily, make a list of things you would like to have and begin giving them to yourself, giving gifts to others and yourself, enjoy giving to others, appreciate your own kind thoughts or actions, thanking yourself if you are generous, say "I love you" to yourself, appreciating yourself as a child using childhood photos as prompts, journal—emphasizing unconditional love and acceptance and meditate to practice being present to yourself. Other authors suggest an approach of *self-gifting* can be to create individual meaningful *self-gifts*, be they large or small, but as a pre-contemplated prioritised plan over a set period initially (Kirshenbaum, 2000). In this case, useful considerations include happiest memories, early dreams and aspirations, identification of what is enjoyed and potential role models, areas for change and improvement, identification of self likes and dislikes, as well as a recognition of important and least important parts of life.

Some of these strategies could be referred to as self-affirmations (Steele, 1988) and have been successfully used in broader contexts such as promoting healthier living and behaviours (Harris & Napper, 2005; Epton & Harris, 2008). An example of a self-affirmation task used in these contexts might involve choosing among a set of values (e.g. Forgiveness, Loyalty, Honesty) for the one that is considered most personally important and then writing a short statement about why this value is significant or influential in life. Promoting self-affirmation in this way appears to act as a buffer to any potentially subsequent threatening information, allowing a more open and less defencive manner of processing (McQueen & Klein, 2006). This occurs not necessarily by repairing the threat to the *Self*, but by using an alternative strategy of regaining an overall positive self-evaluation (Zhao & Nan, 2010).

For those LE, and there are some, that may feel that any attempts at self-affirmation would be pointless since they are in a state of total opposite, for example, in the case of depression. It is useful to note that even depression can be adaptive in limerence. Notably, Fisher (2004) suggests that depression, as it occurs following a lost love, may in fact have a biological beneficial purpose in that it conserves energy and signals the need for social support from others, as well as helping to avoid in making poor choices next time. Unquestionably, for the LE suffering depression, the path ahead might be particularly difficult but by no means insurmountable.

At whatever stage the LE are in recovery, there is likely to be a useful and meaningful way forward. But wherever the LE are, one theme to be addressed appears to be very significant and common, and that is the issues of past and present *attachment issues*. In terms of past attachments, some LE find discussing issues with parents, siblings, or other childhood figures helpful, whereas others say it is simply too painful or generally unwise to revisit. Certainly, there is a theme for older LE that *time is running out* to take on such a task, given the advancing age and associated health problems of parents in particular. For some, it seems discussing issues of attachment with those involved can be a *cure-all pill* or a *poison* for others, and to what extent either applies it has to be a personal call. In terms of present day attachments, some LE describe how they choose to live with and maybe manage better or cherish more, but other attachments LE may give up on and save the pain. It seems that limerence can show up LE's own problems but may also highlight many others' problems more clearly too. Ultimately, in limerence, LE are often faced with one attachment that is likely to need to go or at least transform into a more manageable and less destructive kind, being that to the LO. To this extent, it is useful to visualise attachment as sticky gum between two fingers, in that it can be stretched and pulled so it gets longer, thinner, and baggier, until eventually one day, it finally breaks.

An alternative view regarding attachment is provided by Bradshaw (1990) who recommends that if you want to change the present, as opposed to consideration to outward attachments, it can be useful to change the core material or inner child. He suggests this could involve going back through developmental stages and finishing any unfinished business. For example, by grieving any unmet needs in order that energy is not frozen. He suggests that repression and shaming of emotions can be common and this *original pain* needs to be reexperienced and expressed, or under the influence of ego defences it risks being *acted outward* or *inward*. He advocates validating childhood experiences and using grief as a healing process combined with sharing the *story*, letter writing, and affirmations, applied to the childhood stages of infant, toddler, preschool child, school child, and adolescence. Thereafter, it is possible to champion or parent the inner child with nurture and teaching in a timely and sequential manner. This may involve forgiveness, connecting recalled childhood traumas with current strengths in order to create new positive anchors, or creating new disciplines such as recognizing feelings are okay, but there are also times for delayed gratification and responsibly. Lastly, he recommends consideration to new rules such as regulating expression of feelings and correcting shame-based thinking. Ultimately, he suggests it is possible to create a wonder child or *Imago Dei* as "the part of you that bears a likeness to your creator" (p251) as a different *Self* with a larger vision.

Therapeutic Writing

Baumeister & Wotman (1992) suggest that *making stories* is facilitated by a *need for meaning,* which includes finding purpose, creating self-efficacy, seeking to justify actions within social values, and continuing self-worth. The drive toward developing coherent explanation regarding the feelings, thoughts and events associated with unusual experiences and a desire for some sense of acceptance, has long been recognised by the wider scientific and health community, such as in the case of developing illness representations when unexpected health issues arise (Petrie & Weinman, 1997).

Some have specifically advocated a role for expression of such *stories*, through therapeutic talking and/or writing exercises, be they shared or private (i.e. a letter that is not sent) (Halpern, 1982; Pennebaker, 1997; Lepore & Smyth, 2002). Indeed, creation and expression of *stories* has been found to promote health enhancing effects and to protect against the potentially health damaging effects of nondisclosure. For example, collectively, it has been found that the process of creating and expressing *stories* can be cathartic, allows vague emotions to be considered and labeled, helps identify goals, review feedback, and plan adjustment to behaviours, frees up working memory space, reduces the frequency and intensity of rumination, and ultimately has even been associated with improvements in clinical markers, such as blood pressure and immune functioning (Pennebaker, 1997). Lepore & Greenberg (2002) specifically reviewed the effects of expressive writing in people who had recently experienced a relationship breakup and found, compared to a control group, there were less reports of upper respiratory infections, tensions, and fatigue, etc.

A significant number of LE express how they have been inspired to use many different forms of writing as part of the limerent process. However, not all would advocate the use of writing, with Tennov (1999) warning that journal writing in particular can act to intensify and prolong the experience. There is some evidence for this in the aforementioned therapeutic writing studies, given that many advocate writing for recovery as involving structured and prompted writing sessions, such as writing for set times on predetermined days in order to encourage focus, as well as facilitating the need for closure on the given topic, rather than unstructured writing techniques (Lepore & Smyth, 2002).

Tennov (1999) noted how some LE used a writing based strategy of record keeping for their physical sensations or ruminative thinking, in order to analyse the data for potential significant triggers and patterns, the latter hopefully demonstrating improvement or at least diminishing events. Such a strategy could be a cognitive approach, in that the situation could be reviewed in the knowledge of non-limerence so as to see more clearly the lack of hope. More elaborate versions of this strategy might include creating a timeline trajectory, which included events that actually happened in regard to the limerent episode. The timeline might include: what events actually happened between the LE and LO, as well as what behaviours and associated feelings may have occurred. Such a strategy as this may be useful in attempts to work out *what actually happened* and then for reevaluating the *signs*, labeling emotions, identifying triggers that become either negative or positive, gaining better overall perspective, or for considering where (if any) is the blame. That is to say, some LE do seem to be driven to consider what mistakes were made by both parties, presumably so that lessons can be learned about the present to make it the best it can be, and lessons can be learned for the future too. Thus, LE describe how they have used such written timelines to re-assess the past, review the present and to make predictions. Another clear benefit of such timelines is, in keeping with other forms of therapeutic writing, simply no longer having to save emotions, thoughts, and events as memories, the LE has the capacity to free up working memory space and, as such, potentially reduce the frequency and intensity of ruminations (Lepore, 1997; Pennebaker, 1997; Lepore & Smyth, 2002).

Virtual Support Networks
Currently, there are numerous online support groups, blogs, and information resources regarding both limerence specifically, as well as related subjects such as unrequited love. Unquestionably, all of these e-resources are useful, particularly for LE who have not chosen to disclose their experience to anyone, such that they might find some virtual support at least. Virtual friendships and advice can be equally as rewarding as real life ones, indeed perhaps more so since virtual relationships can be confidential and have the potential at least to be accessed and developed as the LE dictates, that is to say LE can chime in or just observe, friend or

defriend as required. However, having said that, even virtual relationships require social skill, and LE can inadvertently (or not) offend others or disagree. To this extent, some LE prefer to use or complement online support with a different strategy, that of enlisting some form of professional help.

Psychological Therapy

Tennov (1999) was not an advocate of psychotherapy in her time. Specifically, she gave numerous examples of problems in therapy for LE, in particular those associated with women clients and the occurrence of transference, whereby the LE inadvertently transfers the limerence from their current LO to the therapist instead. Thus, she warns "I have come to believe that psychotherapy would be dangerous to the limerently inclined woman" (Tennov, 1999. p203). Indeed, therapeutic setting or not, Tennov (2005) suggested that it is probably best not to indulge the LE in excessively talking about their LO. Unlike Tennov, Bowlby (1988) was an advocate of psychotherapy and described the therapeutic implications of attachment theory, which could be relevant to limerence, as relating to five tasks. These tasks involve using the therapist as a secure base, exploring views about current and past internal working models of attachment, exploring the therapeutic relationship itself, linking past experiences to presents ones and questioning current belief systems with an aim to feel, think and act anew.

Fortunately, current LE often do seek professional therapeutic support, including a variety of styles and genres. Key modalities of therapy include

Psychoanalytic, Psychodynamic, Psychosynthesis, Cognitive Behavioural, Transpersonal, Hypnotherapy, Acceptance and Commitment and Mindfulness or Compassionate Focused, to name but a few.

Psychoanalytic and psychodynamic therapists use a method of *talk therapy* whereby clients are facilitated to disclose patterns or events that may be relevant to their current situation. Based on the work of Sigmund Freud, Carl Jung, Alfred Adler, Melanie Klein, and others, these therapists regard childhood events and associated unconscious feelings, thoughts, and motivations as influential and even causal to subsequent behaviours including mental illness. Therapists can offer an empathetic, confidential, and nonjudgmental environment, where clients can safely express their current feelings. Some therapists also incorporate hypnotherapy into client sessions. Psychodynamic therapists also regard developing awareness of unconscious processes as they may affect current life situations, but tend to use a shorter, more targeted approach (McWilliams, 2004; Jacobs, 2010). A limitation of some psychoanalytical and psychodynamic therapists is that their aim is to facilitate an understanding of the problem, but not necessarily a way forward.

Cognitive-Behavioural Therapy is also a talking-based therapy, built on the work of Albert Ellis, Aaron Beck, and others, which focuses on identifying and changing any dysfunctional emotions, behaviours, and cognitive processes by using goal-oriented procedures. Therapy can be short and targeted using the therapist as a guide.

The approach can be used successfully with a wide range of problems and is often employed in modifying behaviours that have been reinforced over time including phobias (Briers, 2009; Westbrook, Kennerley & Kirk, 2011). However, with such deep problem behaviours as limerence, this therapy, which focuses on clear thinking and involves challenging questioning by the therapist, needs to be used sensitively and compassionately and over a longer rather than shorter time span.

Whereas, Transpersonal Psychotherapy, based on the Humanistic approach and the work of William James and Abraham Maslow and others, regards self-development beyond the personal into human and spiritual encompassments. This relatively new discipline gives consideration to the mind-body interaction, beyond ego development and significant experience and can use positive influence, rather than defences, in identifying, facilitating, and shifting toward higher processes (Rowan, 2005). Psychosynthesis, based on Roberto Assagiolo, includes the experience of self and spiritual awareness, with embracing diversity and social integration, plus themes of center, balance, and free will (Assagiolo, Girelli & Bartoli, 2008) and can be integrated with Transpersonal Therapy.

Hypnotherapy offers an opportunity for the LE to relax in a safe environment, and for their own manipulative thoughts to be discarded and replaced by helpful ones. Gestalt and Neuro-Linguistic Programming techniques can also be used with hypnotherapy so that when the LE is feeling vulnerable they unconsciously strengthen their emotional and psychological defences. In some countries, it is vitally important that a therapist offering hypnotherapy can show evidence of professional training, such as a three year course from an accredited college.

Acceptance and Commitment and Mindfulness Therapy, a type of person-centered therapy, is based on the work of Steven Hayes, Carl Rogers, Linehan, Kanter and Comtois, and others and involves a process of acceptance and change, with unwanted thoughts and feelings being *let go*, together with developing a greater awareness of being in the *present moment* and in actions that have personal value. It includes the theme of acceptance as labeling (thoughts, feelings, and sensations), letting go, accepting (separate self from thoughts and thoughts from referents), as well as being mindful (open and compassionate) and committed to act. Acceptance and mindfulness can combine and overlap during the process. Also relevant is the role of proceeding or *willingness* to fully experience and to act, as alternatives to anxiety and rumination, and of the need for *exposure* to practice willingness (Lejeune, 2007). Compassionate Therapy, based on Paul Gilbert, involves encouraging and developing compassion, especially in relation to processes of guilt, shame, and self-criticism. He notes systems of threat, drive, and affiliation, the latter being therapeutically key for development, given the role of an evolutionary adaptive attachment process, which can be regulatory. Developing compassionate self-identity can be particularly useful in association with traumatic memories and can involve numerous techniques from imagery to letter writing (Gilbert, 2009; 2010).

Tennov (1999) states how psychologist Ellis suggests that LE should give up their "irrational and damaging philosophies" (p265) toward a preferred state of acceptance, and certainly, LE report that they have used therapy in an attempt to do just that. Indeed, of the many therapies described above, while all feature as useful to some or other degree, often, LE currently recognise a preference toward Acceptance and Commitment and Mindfulness or Compassionate Focused approaches. Moreover, it is well known that possibly the most important factor in any successful therapy is a good working relationship between client and therapist, and this has to include respect as a two-way stream.

Whatever particular modality is used, Tennov (1999) would support the idea that therapists should, at onset, make clear to clients that transference might occur, to generate a realistic image, and to explain that it would be essential to terminate the therapy should it occur. However, it is likely that, having been warned of the specter of transference, a client will be able to recognise any risky thoughts and firmly reject them. Certainly, there are now many procedures rightfully in place to protect both clients and therapists, whatever their specific practice. We recognised that at this time, while some therapists have heard of the subject of limerence, many have not, and certainly, there seems to be few professional practitioners currently using the term. Indeed, at this point, there is still no recognised therapeutic framework with which to diagnose or treat LE within the professional community. Clearly, what would also be useful is if a resource network regarding limerence were readily available.

Pharmaceutical Therapy

Some LE find that pharmaceutical interventions may be useful in their recovery. They report using a wide range of different treatments, relating perhaps to their primary symptoms, as well as personal preference and tolerance, together presumably with their clinicians recommendation. Fisher (2004) describes how since love is associated with a depletion of the neurotransmitter serotonin, the use of Selective Serotonin Reuptake Inhibitors might be recommended in a low dose for depression and higher doses for obsession and compulsion. In addition to dissipating problematic limerent symptoms, these drugs can also stimulate nerve cell growth in the hypothalamus (which is associated with memory), thus potentially reversing stress-induced harm (Goode, Peterson & Pollack, 2002). However, the side effects are numerous from weight gain to sexual dysfunction and apathy, and as such, it may be useful to consider a supplement of dopamine elevating drugs, which do not tend to confer similar side effects (Rosenthal, 2000). Lastly, to inhibit the breakdown of plummeting levels of phenylethylamine following rejection, Tallis (2004) suggests that Monoamine Oxidase Inhibitors might help. LE specifically note the common use of depression and anxiety drugs, generically these include: Duloxetine, Escitalopram/Citalopram, Paroxetine, with drugs for rumination including Paroxetine.

In addition to these conventional treatments, some LE try homeopathic remedies such as Natrum Muriaticum-sea salt, especially useful where the limerent episode involves starvation or rejection, with such remedies always best prescribed and monitored by a recognised homeopathic practitioner. Alternatively, some LE recommend eating chocolate as a drug of choice. Indeed, chocolates can contain stimulant chemicals similar to phenylethylamine, which, as stated, can plummet after rejection. But unfortunately, the use of chocolate to this end is controversial, since in general, insufficient quantities and metabolism issues make its clinical effectiveness negligible (Tallis, 2004).

Avoiding Reescalation & Reoccurrence

Where the limerent experiences have been particularly painful, LE are often very motivated to prevent reescalation or reoccurrence of the episode. For reescalation avoidance, main strategies are associated with recognizing boundaries and the use of NC or LC, as discussed. As a measure of reescalation, some LE become vigilant of the extent to which they are slipping back into excessive ruminating about their LO. LE may notice a pattern whereby the more they try to stop ruminating, the more intrusive LO thoughts occur. This can result in a sense of losing control, allowing for more rumination. To this extent, as previously stated, some LE have described how, rather than attempts to stop rumination or the *cold turkey* technique, they use a strategy of allowing a time limit for obsessing or wallowing (which ever best applies at the time) and then gradually cutting the allocated time back. At least in this case, any sense of personal control can be preserved.

A further key theme regarding reescalation and the need to avoid broader LO cues is to avoid *euphoric recall* whereby previous particularly pleasurable moments are remembered. So some LE describe that while they do allow short periods of some rumination about their LO, they limit the type of activity. That is, rumination about events occurring between the LE and LO or *signs* might be permitted, but not *special moments* or fantasy thoughts. Furthermore, in order to avoid too many rumination episodes being triggered, some LE avoid certain places, activities, and cues for their LO (not easy when they have become *omnipresent* at least in an imaginary sense). In this regard, cues that hold particularly high risk significance are music or certain songs. LE note as part of the limerent episode that a *soundtrack* emerges where particular songs remind them of their LO and associated events. This is not at all unexpected since, at limerence heights, almost anything can cue LO rumination, and many songs specifically regard subjects akin to the limerent experience.

Tennov (1999) reported how some LE used music to soothe, and undoubtedly, there may be a role for its use in this respect, but often, LE find they need to change their music genre to avoid the cues. For example, *"I can't listen to any of my playlist, for now I just have to listen to music without words, else every word of my songs seems to be about her or us" (Undisclosed Author)*. Even beyond the problems of linkage of song themes or words to specific limerent experiences, recent research suggests that music in all its forms may have particular significance since it can be deeply associated to attachments. Specifically, there is a prenatal ability to recognise prosody in speech (i.e. rhythm), through to humming lullabies and shared singing such that music is socially communicative (Rock, Trainor & Addison, 1999; Siegler, DeLoache & Eisenberg, 2011). Recently, the biological foundations of musical perception and production have been linked to those of attachment, with the authors stating "We have shown for the first time at a molecular level that music perception has an attachment creating impact" (Liisa, Päivi Onkamo, Raijas, Karma & Järvelä, 2009).

Avoidance of reescalation of limerence is also achieved best, LE report, when avoiding excessive alcohol or recreational drug use. Basically, anything that can reduce inhibition has been cited as dangerous firstly for switching down conscious control and secondly for switching up inclination toward radical honesty, which, when not *under the influence,* would be regarded abhorrent. It is, of course, the case that often LE advocate the need for rest and relaxation at times, and if versions of intoxication achieve this, then *c'est la vie*, but notably, not even the most depressed of LE would advocate this as a long-term strategy.

In terms of reoccurrence to a new LO, LE describe how, once triggered, there may be no more than a few weeks to stop the escalation, with some serial LE describing how they realise the chemical process is occurring. Tennov (2005) recognised the problems of attempting to avoid limerence and advocated that "Mentally, if not physically, you must run away and not give in to budding limerent thoughts" (p12).

Reoccurrence is a particular issue among LE, who feel that they have yet to come to terms with whatever foundations and coexisting conditions personally apply. For example, those that have yet to address attachment issues might support the proposition that *attachment hunger* can be unhealthily played out as an addiction that can out-fuel limerence (Halpern, 1982) and, by extension, presumably create susceptibility to fall again. In spite of the difficulties, Fisher (2004) advocates that we can control the yearnings of love. Specifically, she notes that the prefrontal cortex in the brain is capable of exerting control over the amygdala and other evolutionarily older systems, including the limbic system that generate emotions and impulses. Often for LE, along with consideration to self-acceptance, they also describe the capacity to control and use their limerence experiences in insightful learning.

Both reescalation and reoccurrence may be best achieved having given thorough consideration to all the factors that may underpin the limerent experience from its biological foundations, predispositions, personal circumstance, and attachment issues, through to the role that processes such as addiction, obsession, or anxieties may take, particularly as they relate to (1) the *imagined* LO (2) the *real* LO and (3) the *physiological activity* that underpin them. That is to say, just as a smoker may seek to first understand their thoughts and feelings about smoking, then put in place external barriers (e.g. putting away cigarette packets, lighters, and ashtrays), they will also at some point need to come to terms with bodily sensations associated with the craving. Thus, a multitude of factors will often need to interplay in order to modify the complexity of thoughts, feelings, sensations, and behaviours that typify any experience, and so it is with limerence also.

Notably, LE describe the development of insight as a key process in the limerent experience, and some use a variety of therapeutic interventions to assist in limerence recovery. Obviously, the range and type of interventional method is LE specific, with some choosing to utilise a few or all methods concurrently, to differing degrees, and at different times during the limerence trajectory. Whatever the precise journey taken, encouragingly, often LE come to regard the experience as potentially inspirational in many ways.

Chapter 6

Practical Strategies Part 4: Inspirational Aspects of Limerence

One of the key issues in limerence as Tennov (1999) points out is that, "the longing for a partner is so intense as to be experienced as a necessity" (p141). But as the LO as a focus of self-identity is replaced with alternative beliefs and values in keeping with a more rational reality-centered living, the potential benefits of the experience can be exploited. These benefits often include improving health and physical appearance, but also extend to acquiring new skills and knowledge (ranging from self-awareness and development to learning an instrument or starting a new job or course of study), through to impacting on artistic expression, meditation, yoga, martial arts, and philosophies. In these terms then, LE come to reconnect and reintegrate mind and body. For LE, limerence can be inspirational.

<u>Food</u>
Limerence can be an extreme stressor, which can increase comfort food intake and result in associated weight gain, with cortisol tending to increase craving for foods high in fat, sugar, and salt (Hargreaves, 2012). For those LE that already had a self-defined distorted relationship with food, it is unsurprising that limerence

can amplify these difficulties. Along with overeating, some LE describe a cycle of food as a reward or punishment (overeat or don't eat) and in these cases, if the cycle is pervasive, some LE try to switch the overeating part to healthier choices at least. However, by far, the majority of the select LE cases available report that the desire to enhance physical appearance can cause them to move toward healthier food choices with some starting new diet routines.

Fisher (2004) advocates that, in love recovery, it is best to avoid high sugar, stimulant foods, and those generally drugs related. In limerence, the trend toward healthier diets can be useful to simultaneously stabilise mood, prevent cravings, and enhance physical appearance. Such healthier diets might include: (1) eating regular meals (especially breakfast) to stabilise blood sugar, boost metabolism, and ensure energy is used effectively, (2) positive mood foods such as Tryptophan (e.g. poultry and oil-rich fish), which is an amino acid necessary for producing serotonin, (3) carbohydrates, vitamins, and minerals to help serotonin uptake in the brain, (4) snacks such as fruit with seeds or yogurt, and lastly, (5) adequate and balanced consumption of omega-3 and omega-6 oil since these are beneficial for general health as well as mood (Hargreaves, 2012).

<u>Exercise</u>
A further consideration in relation to love recovery is the necessity to attempt to redress potentially plummeting levels of dopamine (Fisher, 2004). Exercise is useful since it can increase dopamine in the nucleus

accumbens part of brain, as well as elevating serotonin and endorphins. Exercise can also increase brain-derived neurotropic factor in the hippocampus, associated with memory protecting and generating nerve cells. Furthermore, exercise taken outside has the added benefit of the potential to experience sunlight, which can lift mood by stimulating the brains pineal gland.

Exercise types popular to LE are as diverse as people are themselves including gym related, running, tennis, team sports and all types of dance, from line dancing to ballet. Interestingly, the more mindless versions (e.g. running on treadmills at gyms) remain popular throughout limerence recovery, whereas others that require skill or memory seem to be utilised differently at times, depending on the LE's perceived ability to concentrate. Notably, Tennov (1999) warns that exercise can become versions of self-harm when used excessively to provide relief. Undoubtedly, there is evidence of this as LE seemingly swap one biological high for another, but if a vice must be sought, rather this than say excessive drug use. For example, *"Okay, I was an exercise junkie at first, but after I had run a marathon on the cross trainer and swam a sea in the swimming pool, that's when I knew that recovery was possible".* Certainly, LE describe the realization that it is possible, temporarily at least, to swap an emotional pain for a physical pain, and often LE note their new ability to push through the pain barrier in exercise more fervently than ever before under the influence of limerence. But notwithstanding these factors, at least exercise (when combined with adequate sleep, rest, and recovery) has the potential to increase physical health and well-being and to enhance physical appearance, both useful for increasing self-esteem.

Physical Appearance

Along with the hot baths and personal indulgences Tennov (1999) noted were popular cure attempts for limerence, comes the general theme of the need from LE to invest in physical appearance from hairstyles to fashion. Some take this to extreme and describe a limerence-induced physical appearance enhancing debt! Some LE apparently find themselves making odd or unusual selections, some of which may be enhancing and flattering but others apparently less so. Often, the choices relate to wanting to look in a way that the chosen LO would find attractive with frankly insufficient regard to that which might best suit or fit the LE. To this end, there are examples of LE describing unfortunate choices for hairstyles or fashion, which they come to regret. For example, *"given extensive searching on [social networking site] amongst his closest friends etc., I came to the decision that he probably preferred blonds and set off to remedy my black hair. It turns out blond suits some women but not others...definitely not me. Now I look, LOL ridiculous!"* (Undisclosed Author).

Similarly, there is an overall theme of LE dressing to get attention from their LO and, to this extent, dressing sexually *provocative* comes up, especially for women LE. Indeed, this also includes the theme of items that are not publically noticeable. That is, some LE describe how, in limerence, they invested (some for the first time) in more sexy lingerie. Again, not every LE is perhaps best suited to being a lingerie model, but still the effects of such investments can show to the positive by enhancing body shape through new and hopefully better fitting garments and secondly by altering the way LE feel, especially toward self-esteem and confidence. Whatever the motivation, physical appearance self-enhancements can be a valuable limerent inspiration. Indeed, taking increased personal pride in appearance for some LE may be a relatively novel or long overdue experience. LE appear to concur that so long as enhancing physical appearance is moderated and does not become yet another obsession, which results in unused garments and an unaffordable drain to the bank account, then why not enhance your personal assets, whatever the individual LE perceives them to be.

Artistic Expression

Key themes for recovering from love and its variances also regard that focusing attention and embarking on doing novel things is most relevant, since collectively this can build energy and hope (Fisher, 2004). These sentiments can be coupled with the further view that "love can potentiate hitherto untapped reserves of creativity, and this creativity is often linked with the desire to excel and impress" (Tallis, 2004. p277).

Tennov (1999) recognised that "It appears to be characteristic of the state of limerence that you are inclined to express your feelings in writing" (p160). However, she also noted that given possible feelings of shame and need to remain anonymous, more often limerence expression may be less literal and more often involve alternative mediums. Tennov (2005) herself wrote a number of plays and short stories, and LE can recount lists of other writings (whether originally intended or not) that appear to be limerent related including fiction (e.g. Emily Bronte, Wuthering Heights; Rosemary Sullivan, Labyrinth of Desire), prose (Maya Angelou, New Directions) and poems (Brian Patten, Her Song). Similarly, limerence may be widely reflected in songs (e.g. Dan Wilsons - Secret Smile by Semisonic), films (e.g. Richard Curtis' *Love Actually*, in particular the plot between Mark (Andrew Lincoln) [LE] and Juliet (Keira Knightly) [LO]) and alternative artistic mediums.

It seems that one of the factors some LE find outstanding about the limerent experience is that in spite of the endless process of rumination, there is also an ability to switch off, at least for short periods, and function on complicated tasks, especially if they are in some way initially limerence inspired. Moreover, particularly in the case of starvation and rejection, some LE find they need their art to channel limerence where no other route is available. Certainly, there are those LE that have sought to share their artistic creations with those who were inspirational to them, who then report having found a cool response with the sentiment lost. But no matter, art is what it is for the maker, firstly and significantly. Tennov (1999; 2005) noted that undoubtedly limerence may be inspirational for artistic expression—the good, the bad, the appreciated, and that which is less desired as well.

Acquisition of Knowledge & Skills

Somewhere along the line, LE often describe how they were motivated to focus their attention into doing something new, a strategy theorist of love might advocate (Fisher, 2004). The more organised LE even make a list of new things to do with their lives, hopefully most with achievable targets. This is in keeping with a general theme of the need to keep busy. Versions of keeping busy to LE can be as diverse as they are interesting, including those who take on building and renovation projects, new courses of study through to learning to play new musical instruments. It seems that applying the mind is the key point such as to reduce rumination by way of distraction, but also to utilise the surge of energy in a constructive way. It is outstanding the amount that can be achieved under the influence of limerence in any one day. Furthermore, those activities, where there are objective markers for progress such as grades or levels of achievement, are indispensable for facilitating an often much needed raise to *self-achievement* and associated self-esteem. Interestingly, some LE note that these activities are particularly useful when they rely on self alone, that is unlike in limerence progress, to some degree at least, can be directly related to the LE's chosen input rather than the vagaries of interaction with anyone else. To this extent a sense of *control* can be regained as well.

Meditation

In limerence, as elsewhere, meditation and yoga or martial arts are often used in unison, with some mantras being made love recovery-specific (Fisher, 2004). Specifically, meditation can involve a process of self-regulation or transformation to achieve a mode of consciousness perceived to be beneficial. Various awareness techniques may be involved such as mantras (words or sounds evoking energy/peace), being aware of/observing breathing and mental distractions, visualization, and quietening the mind and/or allowing key focus. Meditation may be performed alone or with others, often sitting, with some using music or a meditation dialogue, as well as beads or other focus objects.

Huber (2010) is an advocate of meditation, suggesting that in meditation you can learn not to resist or to react, and that sitting still with yourself is loving yourself, noting "to sit still in compassionate acceptance is all that is required" (p90). Additionally, Thich, Nhat, Hanh (2009) recommends meditation as practice to be *present* in the *here and now,* with such *mindfulness* enabling contact with beauty, healing, and refreshment, as well as allowing the return to the *Self* and embracement of pain. Similarly, Heaversedge & Halliwell (2012) suggest that mindfulness meditation can help cope with stress, physically heal, and aid in letting go of unhelpful behaviours, as well as enabling relating to others more effectively. They suggest mindfulness encourages an open awareness to both internal and external worlds such that, with practice, events and our reactions to them can be responded to with open-hearted compassion. Specifically, mindfulness can reduce rumination and could be used as a type of "self-parenting" (p89) whereby, through noncritical observation, a secure attachment may be fostered by an *internal good parent*.

Collectively, some LE might describe the role of meditation, yoga, or martial arts and mantras as useful because: *"in limerence, both mind and body are implicated and need to heal", "the process is challenging and requires focus", "it provides a legitimate reason for time away for the Self", "it inspires personal awareness and responsibility for emotions, thoughts, behaviour, and life", "it can be physically calming or create a sense of well-being",* with some noting a form of *"self-hypnosis"* and *"own parenting".* With some LE linking meditation, yoga, martial arts, and mantras to higher spiritual processes in their lives.

Philosophies
At some point in the limerent experience, often LE come to consider subjects such as philosophies. Within these domains, one common theme arises as LE describe that they had perceived their LO to be a type of *soul mate* (Moore, 1995). Some LE believe their LO is a connection from a past life or even a connection from the states between past lives (Newton, 2000).

Some LE perceived the LO as a need to achieve *oneness.* Indeed, Tennov (1999) recognised the role of limerence in achieving a sense of *oneness* such that limerence might be related to love, but in limerence, she notes the feelings are excessive. Many people more generally would recognise that there is a more or less permanent state of unease regarding attaining *oneness,* and that it is a common life theme to attempt to possess things that are unreachable, as in ideas of existentialism philosophy, such as in Jean-Paul Satre's account of *Being and Nothingness* (Satre, 1991).

A further connected theme is that LE often describe a feeling of *emptiness* and a feeling of *separateness* as a form of suffering. Indeed, the theme of becoming emotionally aware as highlighting pain (Zukav & Francis, 2002), or of ego-related suffering or egocentricity *as* suffering (Huber, 2009) and of the ego identification with the pain-body (Tolle, 2001) are all common themes generally, limerence or not. But notably, in relation to limerence, LE often describe how their LO may have *temporarily filled the feeling of emptiness in their lives,* at least for a while. For example, *"With my LO, I felt complete, but I am mostly over it now. My new fear is how to avoid falling back into nothingness as a consequence." (Undisclosed Author).* Now clearly, often for LE the process is a painful journey, but by no means is the outcome always negative. Indeed, Huber (2010) notes that a form of *emptiness* can be inadvertently induced for people who are attempting a process of giving up self-hate, such that there is then a tendency to fill up with distractions creating a cycle of *emptiness*. But she notes that *emptiness* in these terms can be defined as involving "limitless possibility" (Huber, 2009. p215).

It seems that the limerent experience can make such feelings salient and, as such, also provide an opportunity to review and potentially alter thinking. Mostly, LE do this in regard to their LO specifically, but some come to do this by taking what could be described as a further step by totally reevaluating and/or developing the *Self*. Thus, often in the limerent episode, some LE describe an awareness that they need to *get back to* themselves. But interestingly, this is the point that some LE seem to take a further step in relation to the *Self*, in that they find that they can't *get back*. That is to say that it is not possible to view limerence as a circle, rather it is a journey and its ending, or at least its trajectory, will leave the LE significantly changed from the person that they perceived themselves to be before it occurred. In this sense limerence describes a journey as a move towards a more conscious and *Authentic Self*.

Some LE describe limerence in religious terms, for example by stating that limerence feels like a religion in itself. Some LE apparently feel that at some point in the episode they temporarily *traded* their God for their LO. The theme of being in religious crisis when the limerence occurred is common as is the use of prayer for coping during the episode. Thus, limerence seems to have a role in questioning faith, potentially modifying, changing faith, or making faith stronger. In this respect, limerence, as is often the case with unexpected life events, can be referred to as an *epiphany* or *realization*, which may facilitate numerous and varied life changes. Clearly, for the LE whom religion features or for those who are interested in religiosity, limerence can provide a catalyst for reevaluation, change, or new beginnings.

At some point in the limerent experience, LE describe the need to review *what happened,* and this can sometimes result in the proportioning of blame. Such blaming process can be widespread and include the *Self*, *Others*, *Gods* etc. Specifically, as is pertinent to the limerent experience, blaming previous attachments issues or the LO may be most common, but mostly LE recognise that blame is rarely a useful way forward.

Certainly whatever part an LO played (if any) in the limerence episode, the remedy was never their responsibility so there can be no blame to be apportioned there.

Notwithstanding the fact that blame and anger are likely to be a common and potentially adaptive part of the grief process of recovery, it is worth noting that, as a continued life theme, Huber (2009) suggests a preferable state of compassionate awareness might be advocated with the keys being to pay attention to everything, believing nothing (avoiding assumptions), and take nothing personally. Poignantly, Huber (2010) states "living from compassion for ourselves gives us each the loving parent we've always wanted" and that "It doesn't matter what happened then. All that matters is what happens now" (Huber, 2010. p206; p217).

Similarly, LE also describe the recognition that they need to forgive themselves for falling into limerence and that they also need to try to forgive their LO for not reciprocating, for being overwhelmed, frightened, less than honest, or less than kind in particular. For some LE, coming to considerations of forgiveness is seen as a marker of progress through the limerent episode. For example, *"I have had to work on forgiving my LO cos I can now see I depleted his ego (he has many younger women adorers than me). There was confusion etc. We both messed up, turns out we are both human. I made an error in falling into limerence with him, and he handled it less than brilliantly, but I realise that it is probably not easy for anyone to become the temporary obsession of a mad person, such as I was! Interestingly, where I used to want to disclose my limerent feelings to my LO, I now have the urge to say sorry instead! I think this must be some sort of progress." (Undisclosed Author).* But note that even for these LE, forgiveness is not the same as then tolerating unkind behaviour or rudeness from a LO, rather it is just an acceptance that the LO are whoever they are and give what they give, whether it meets the needs of an LE or not. Certainly, if an LO set their boundaries to exclude the LE and, in so doing, appear arrogant, then that requires forgiveness. Similarly, if an LO is weird or awkward in the presence of the LE, as may well be the case if they (1) know they are adored and (2) don't, can't, or daren't reciprocate, then that also will benefit from forgiveness. Ultimately, it seems LE recognise that there is progress and empowerment in forgiveness.

In the limerence trajectory, the theme of the need to develop self-esteem, self-acceptance, and self-love often become central, together with the recognition that there has been a pervasive *sense of emptiness,* which the *imagined* and *real* LO may have temporarily covered. To this extent, the perceived need to *fill the space* may persist, such that limerence can become an epiphany of an emotional, intellectual, or spiritual awakening (such as developing the use of meditation or relaxation techniques, or consideration toward mindfulness, religiosity, and spiritual experiences). Even though, as the need to *regain control* and *dis-entrapment* play out, some LE report how they may have initially taken recovery strategies to excess, most do achieve a happier medium in the end. Ultimately, it seems limerence may be health inspiring, insightful, empowering, and enlightening. Limerence can become the gift of energy and inspiration, which LE learn to harness.

Intentionally or not, knowingly or not, however temporary or not, LE voices might thank LO for the following insights:

Boundaries (mine and others) need to be respected.

It is worthy to increase self-esteem & self-love.

Expectations can be met about how to be desired and treated.

There is potential for personal strength and self-control.

LO improved feelings of sexuality.

It may not be possible to know why a particular LO is selected, but you can identify some triggers.

Limerence is a tendency that I have, which I can learn to manage.

Adoration sometimes seeks to replay and/or heal childhood traumas.

Limerence is an escapism, like drinking alcohol or shopping.

Limerence showed that hard inner work was needed.

Real life relationships require work.

Happiness is within me.

Limerence gave the opportunity to reevaluation relationships including considering whether to stay or go.

Compassionate awareness is necessary.

It's okay to feel strongly for another person, whatever your personal circumstances.

It is possible to love again.

There is no need for shame.

Limerence taught me not to resist but to watch and be present in the moment.

Life can be good, unique things can still happen, not everything is preplanned.

Recovery is possible, even from the darkest of places.

Limerence allowed me to reconnect my mind & body in a healing way.

There is a need to forgive self and others.

The shifting sands of limerence was a much needed epiphany to my life.

Limerence showed me the need to love myself firstly.

Limerence has enabled me live more consciously and authentically.

Conclusion

In Tennov's words, she stated that "How pleasant or painful [limerence] turns out to be in any given instance depends on force of circumstance" (Tennov, 2005. p293) and that "Although my studies have not found a way for limerents to manage the course of limerence according to their individual volition, or even how to cure it once it has taken hold, surely we are closer to imposing our intelligence on the course of our lives than we were when limerence was believed to be entirely under the spell of magic or other supernatural influences" (Tennov, 1999. p274).

Certainly, we hope that as information about and sources of recovery for limerence become more readily available, the course of limerence will become more manageable and definitely less destructive, such that LE can *regain personal control and dis-entrapment to the condition,* as well as being more able to *create and make sense of their story,* factors which may be essential in moving on psychologically and literally toward a *better place.*

In consideration to the potential biological foundations and preexisting or coexisting conditions, as well as complicated interrelations of triggers relating to any one LO in particular, such insight has to be invaluable in the process of understanding the limerence condition. Additionally, Lewis et al (2001) asserts that "Who we are and who we become depends, in part, on whom we

44), and in limerence, there does appear to be estionable theme of the potential influence of achment and bonding figures to subsequent limerent experience, but hopefully, these issues need not *inevitably* produce misplaced and inappropriate attachments of the future.

In the process of recovery, factors such as differentiating between the *imagined* vs the *real* LO and the *physiological activity* that underpin them become salient, as does learning to refocus thinking away from the LO and onto the *Self*. Similarly identifying and modifying behaviours around the LO and others involved may be vital, especially those that are related to issues of boundaries, contact, and disclosure. Notably, given both the commonality and diversity of the limerent experience a one-fix solution is not obvious. Though certainly LE describe the development of insight and the use of interventions, be they self-directed, therapeutic, or pharmaceutical, as beneficial.

Importantly, not all see limerence as a mental illness, though many would recognise the potential issues of addiction, obsessive compulsions, and even free floating anxieties and depression temporarily fixated. Similarly, not all seek immediate and total cure, indeed many will harness the vast and exhaustive benefits that a limerent experience may generate and that have resulted in multiple expressions in literature and art. Ultimately, there is a wealth of evidence that limerence can be health inspiring, insightful, empowering, and enlightening.

In consideration of the LO, it is recognised that the experience can be ego enhancing or depleting. Often there tends to be an element of push and pull, mixed messages and confusion, and sometimes even fear. Since to find that you have become the recipient of an unrequited adoration is not a comfortable place to be. Thus, if it should come to pass that a LE finds themselves as someone else's LO, as of course it sometimes might, one would hope that at least these LE (if they are not interested in reciprocation) might show good practice in being ethical and honest, eliminating any doubt, and setting boundaries, since they themselves have no excuse of *scriptlessness* with which to defend incompetence or uncompassionate treatment of their adorers. Since those who have been a LE and/or those who have read this or other accounts must surely know the experience all too well and, as such, would be highly motivated to save others the pain.

Controversially, it is discussed as to the relative merits of whether LE can remain or indeed become friends with their LO, with the majority of expertise seeming to suggest that friendships merely prolongs suffering, but our hope is that, at some point in the limerent trajectory, friendship might be achievable, notwithstanding a likely period of NC or LC while necessary adjustments are made. For LE, being friends with their LO will likely involve particular skills of limerence management and special vigilance to issues such as boundaries. Certainly, what will help enormously is if the LE had the good luck to have selected an LO who is emotionally mature and fundamentally kind. Either way, we suggest that friendships between LE and their LO are probably best placed to succeed when the LE has successfully taken a personal journey such that they can now sit in quiet acceptance.

For LE who find that they need to (or have to) stay in contact with their LO, it is at least hoped that a modus vivendi might be reached (i.e. way of living for disputing parties). Indeed, LE may well discover that their LO are not entirely the *God or Goddess* like person they were made out to be! Whatever they really are, though, LE are wise to consider that in their presence and influence there may always be a risk of falling back into heightened limerence again. The key may be in identifying the potential triggers of any particular LO in an attempt to ensure that similar triggers will not succumb again.

Ultimately, it seems that there may be biological foundations in the limbic roots of attachments, attraction, and adoration in limerence, but it is possible to resist and indeed even benefit from the effects. With insight and internal work, it is entirely feasible to regain control and dis-entrapment to the condition and to achieve rational reality–centered living that can harness the inspirational aspects of limerence into a journey towards a more authentic self. For Limerent Experiencers, the way forward can be one of self-love, forgiveness, and compassionate acceptance.

References

Abraham, C. Sheeran, P. (2003) Acting on Intentions: The Role of Anticipated Regret. British Journal of Social Psychology, *42,* 495-511.

Acevedo, B. P., Aron, A., Fisher, H. E., Brown, L. L. (2012) Neural Correlates of Long Term Romantic Love. Social Cognition and Affective Neuroscience. 7 2 145-159

Ainsworth, M. D. S. (1967) Infancy in Uganda; Infant Care and the Growth of Attachment. Maryland. John Hopkins Press.

Ainsworth, M. D. S. (1973) The Development of Infant-Mother Attachment. In Caldwell,. Riccuti, H. (Eds) Review of Child Development Research. 3. Chicago. University of Chicago Press.

Ainsworth, M. D. S., Blehar, M. C., Waters, E., Wall, S. (1978) Patterns of Attachment: A Psychological Study of the Strange Situation. New Jersey. Erlbaum.

American Psychiatric Association. (2000). *Diagnostic and statistical manual of mental disorders* (4th ed., text revision.). Washington, DC: Author.

American Psychiatric Association. (2013). *Diagnostic and statistical manual of mental disorders* (5th ed.). Arlington, VA: American Psychiatric Publishing.

Angelou, M. (1994) Wouldn't Take Nothing for My Journey Now. London. Virago Press.

Assagiolo, R., Girelli, M. L., Bartoli, S. (2008) Transpersonal Development: The Dimension Beyond Psychosynthesis. Scotland. Inner Way Productions/ Smiling Wisdom.

Banker, R. (2010) Socially Prescribed Perfectionism and Limerence in Interpersonal Relationships
M.A., University of New Hampshire, 99.

Baumeister, R. F. Wotman, S. R. (1992) Breaking Hearts: Two Sides of Unrequited Love. New York. The Guilford Press.

Benoit, D., Parker, K. C. H. (1994) Stability and Transmission of Attachment Across Three Generations. Child Development 65 1444-1456

Berne, E. (2010) Games People Play. London. Penguin Books.

Blanton, B. (2003) Radical Honesty. Virginia. Sparrow Hawk.

Bowlby, J. (1969) Attachment and Loss. Attachment. Vol 1. New York. Basic Books.

Bowlby, J. (1973) Attachment and Loss. Vol 2. Separation. New York. Basic Books.

Bowlby, J. (1980) Attachment and Loss. Vol 3. Loss, Sadness and Depression. New York. Basic Books.

Bowlby, J. (1988) A Secure Base: Clinical Applications of Attachment Theory. Routledge. London.

Bradley, N. M., Miccoli, L., Escrig, Ma. A., Lang, P. J. (2008) The Pupils as a Measure of Emotional Arousal. *Psychophysiology*. 45 4 602-607

Bradshaw, J. (1990) Homecoming: Reclaiming Your Inner Child. Bantom Books. New York.

Briers, S. (2009) Brilliant Cognitive Behavioural Therapy. Harlow. Pearson.

Bronte, E (1992) Wuthering Heights. Hertfordshire. Wordsworth Classic.

Calef, V., Weinshal, E. M. (1981) Some Clinical Consequences of Introspection: Gaslighting. Psychoanalytic Quarterly. 50 44-67

Clark, A. P. (2006) Are the Correlates of Sociosexuality Different for Men and Women? Personality and Individual Differences. 41 7 1321-1327

Curtis, R., Kenworthy, D., Bevan, T., Fellner, E., Hayward, D., Chasin, L. (2003) Love Actually. British Universal Pictures.

Duhigg, C. (2012) The Power of Habit: Why We Do What We Do and How to Change. London. William Heinmann.

Eigen, R., E. (2005) Is it Love or Is it Projection. The Anima/Animus Phenonomen. Accessed 27th October, 2012.
http://www.shadowdance.com/articles/isitloveorprojection.html ;
http://www.empatheticguidance.wordpress.com

Eisenberger, N. I., Lieberman, M. D. (2004) Why Rejection Hurts: A common Neural Alarm System for Physical and Social Pain. Trends in Cognitive Psychology. 8 7 294-300

Epton, T., Harris, P. R. (2008) Self-affirmation Promotes Health Behaviour Change. Health Psychology. 27 746-752

Fisher, H. E. (2004) Why We Love; The Nature and Chemistry of Romantic Love. New York. St Martin's Griffin.

Fisher, H. E., Brown, L. L., Aron, A., Strong, G., Mashek, D. (2010) Reward, Addiction and Emotional Regulation Systems Associated with Rejection in Love. Journal of Neurophysiology. 104 1 51-60

Freud, A. (1936) The Ego and the Mechanisms of Defence. New York. International University Press.

George, C., Kaplan, N., & Main, M. (1984) Adult Attachment Interview Protocol. Unpublished Manuscript, University of California. Berkeley.

Gilbert P. (2009) Introducing Compassion-Focused Therapy. Advances in Psychiatric Treatment. 15 199-208.

Gilbert P. (2010) Compassion Focused Therapy. London. Routledge

Glass, S. P. (2004) Not "Just Friends" USA. Free Press.
Gollwitzer, PM. (1999) Implementation Intentions. Strong Effects of Simple Plans. American Psychology. 54 493-503.

Goode, E. M., Peterson, M., Pallock, A. (2002) Anti-depressants, Lift Clouds, but Lose "Miracle Drugs" Label. New York Times. June 30th. In Fisher, H. E. (2004) Why We Love; The Nature and Chemistry of Romantic Love. New York. St Martin's Griffin.

Gorski, T. T. (1993) Getting Love Right: Learning the Choices of Healthy Intimacy. New York. Fireside.
Hall, E. (2012) Lust, Love and Limerence, a short story. E-book.

Halpern, H. (1979) No Strings Attached: A Guide to a Better Relationship with your Grown Up Child. New York. Simon & Schuster. In Halpern (1982) How to Break Your Addiction to a Person. New York. McGraw-Hill Book Company.

Halpern, H. (1982) How to Break Your Addiction to a Person. New York. McGraw-Hill Book Company.

Halpern, H. (2004) How to Break Your Addiction to a Person. New York. Bantam Books.

Hansen, S. R. (2006) Courtship Duration as a Correlate of Marital Satisfaction and Stability. Ph.D. Alliant International University, San Diego, 163.

Hargreaves, J. (2012) Nutrition Therapy Practitioner. Communication 6th November 2012.

Harris, P. R,. Napper, L. (2005) Self-affirmation and the Biased Processing of Threatening Health-risk Information. Personality & Social Psychology Bulletin. 31 1250-1263

Hayne, H. (2004) Infant Memory Development. Implications for Childhood Amnesia. Developmental Review. 24 33-73

Heaversedge, J., Halliwell, E. (2012) The Mindful Manifesto. New York. Hay House Inc.

Horowitz, M. J. (1986) Stress Response Syndromes. New Jersey. Jason Aronson.

Horowitz, M. J., Kaltreider, N. B. (1980) Brief Psychotherapy of Stress Response Syndrome. In Karasu, T. B., Bellak, L. (Eds) Specialised Techniques in Individual Psychotherapy. New York. Brunner Mazel.

Huber, C. (2009) Suffering Is Optional. USA. Keep it Simple books.

Huber, C. (2010) There Is Nothing Wrong With You: Going Beyond Self Hate. USA. Keep it Simple Books.

Jacobs, (2010) Psychodynamic Counselling in Action. London. Sage Publications.

Janoff-Bulman, R. (1992) Shattered Assumptions: Towards a New Psychology of Trauma. New York. Free Press.

Kirshenbaum, M. (2000) The Gift of a Year. New York. Penguin.

Kreppner, J. M., Rutter, M., Becket, C., Castle, J., Colvert, E. (2007) Normality and Impairment Following Profound Early Institutional Deprivation: A Longitudinal Follow-up Into Early Adolescence. Developmental Psychology. 43 4 931-946

Kubler-Ross, E., Kessler, D. (2005) On Grief and Grieving. London. Simon & Schuster.

Leckman, J., & Mayes, L. (1999) Preoccupations and Behaviours Associated with Romantic and Parental Love. Perspective on the Origin of Obsessive-Compulsive Disorder. Child Adolescence Psychiatr Clinical North America. 8 3 635-664.

Leckman, J.F., Mayes, L.C., Feldman, R., Evans, D.W., King, R.A., Cohen, D.J. (1999) Early Parental Pre-occupations and Behaviours and their Possible Relationship to the Symptoms of Obsessive-Compulsive Disorder. Acta Psychiatr Scand Supp. 396. 1-26

Lejeune, C. (2007) The Worry Trap. How to Free Yourself From Worry & Anxiety Using Acceptance & Commitment Therapy. Oakland. New Harbinger Publications.

Lepore, S. J. (1997). Expressive Writing Moderates the Relation Between Intrusive Thoughts and Depressive Symptoms. Journal of Personality and Social Psychology. 73 5 1030-1037.

Lepore, S. J., Greenberg, M. A. (2002) Mending Broken Hearts: Effects of Expressive Writing on Mood, Cognitive Processing, Social Adjustment and Health Following a Relationship Break-Up. Psychology & Theory. 17 5.

Lepore, S. J., Smyth, J. M. (2002) The Writing Cure; How Expressive Writing Promotes Health & Emotional Well Being. Washington. American Psychology Society.

Lewis, M. D. (2005) Bridging Emotion Theory and Neurobiology Through Dynamic Systems Modeling. Behavioural and Brain sciences. 28 169-194

Lewis, T., Amini, F. Lannon, R. (2001) A General Theory of Love. New York. Vintage Books.

Liisa. T., Päivi Onkamo, U., Raijas, P., Karma, K., Järvelä, I. (2009) Musical Aptitude Is Associated with AVPR1A-Haplotypes. *PLoS ONE*, 4 5 Retrieved from on 28th October 2012 from
http://www.sciencedaily.com/releases/2009/05/090526093925.htm

Lorenz, K. Z. (1952) King Zolomens Ring. New York. Cromwell.

Lucas-Thompson, R., Clarke-Stewart, k. A. (2007) Forecasting Friendship: How Marital Quality, Maternal Mood and attachment Security are Linked to Children's Peer Relationships. Journal of Applied Developmental Psychology. 28 499-514

Main, M., Kaplan, N., Cassidy, J. (1985) Security, Infancy, Childhood and Adulthood: A Move to the Level of Representation. Monographs of the Society for Research in Child development. 50 1-2

Main, M., Solomen, J. (1990) Procedures for Identifying Infants as Disorganised/Disorientated During the Ainsworth Strange Situation. In Greenberg, M. T., Cicchetti, D., Cummings, E. M. (Eds) Attachment in Pre-school Years. University of Chicago Press. Chicago.

Masten, A. S. (2007) Resilience in Developing Systems: Progress and Promise as the Forth Wave Rises. Development and Psychopathology. 19 921-930

Mayou, A. (1994) Wouldn't Take Nothing For My Journey Now. London. Virago Press.

McKenna, P., Willbourn, H. (2006) I Can Mend Your Broken Heart. London. Transworld.

McQueen, A., Klein, W. M. P. (2006) Experimental Manipulations of Self-affirmation: A Systematic Review. Self & Identity. 5 4

McWilliams, N. (2004) Psychoanalytic Therapy: A Practitioners Guide. New York. Guilford Press.

Moore, T (1994) Soul Mates; Honoring the Mysteries of Love and Relationships. New York. HarperCollins.

Moore, C. (2008) The Development of Gaze Following. Child Developmental Perspectives. 2 66-70

Morris, D. (1973) Intimate Behaviour. New York. Bantom Books. Cited In Tennov, D. (1999) Love and Limerence; The Experience of Being in Love. New York. Scarborough House.

Mullen, P. E., Pathe, M., Purcell, R. (2000) Stalkers and Their Victims. Cambridge. University Press. In Tallis, F. (2004) Love Sick. London. Random House.

Newton, M. (2000) Destiny of the Souls: New Case Studies of Life Between Lives. Minnesota. Llewllyn Publications.

Nievar, M. A., Becker, B. J. (2007) Sensitivity as a Privileged Predictor of Attachment. A Second perspective on de Wolff and van IJzendoorns Meta-Analysis. Social Development. 17 102-114

Page, S. (1997) How One of You Can Bring the Two of You Together. New York. Broadway Books.

Patten, B. (1991) Love Poems. London. Harper Collins.

Pennebaker, J. W. (1997) Emotional, Disclosure & Health. Washington. American Psychology Association.

Petrie, K. J., Weinman, J. A. (1997) Perceptions of Health and Illness. UK. Harwood Academic Publishers.

Pim, R. (2003). Limerence and its Effects on Perceptions of Attractiveness. B.Sc. Honours thesis, Department of Psychology, McMaster University.

Rock, A. M. L., Trainor, L. J., Addison, T. L. (1999) Distinctive Messages in Infant-directed Lullabies and Play Songs. Developmental Psychology, 35 2 527-534

Rogers, C. (1994) On Becoming a Person. London. Routledge.

Rosenthal, N. E. (2000) The Emotional revolution: How the New Science of Feelings can Transform your Life. New York. Citadel press Books. In Fisher, H. E. (2004) Why We Love; The Nature and Chemistry of Romantic Love. New York. St Martin's Griffin.

Rosse, R. B. (2001) The Love Trauma Syndrome: Free Yourself From the Pain of a Broken Heart. USA. Perseus.

Rothbaum, F., Pott, M., Azuma, H., Miyake, K., Weiz, J. (2000) The Development of Close Relationships in Japan and the United States: Paths of Symbiotic Harmony and Generative Tension. Child Development. 71 1121-1142

Rowan, J. (2005) The Transpersonal: Spirituality in Psychotherapy and Counselling. Hove. Routledge.

Rutter, M. (2006) Implications of Resilience Concepts for Scientific Understanding. Annals of the New York Academy of Sciences. 1094 1-12

Sack, D. (2012) Limerence and the Biochemical Roots of Love Addiction. Huffington Post. Retrieved on 7th October, 2012, http://www.huffingtonpost.com/david-sack-md/limerence_b_1627089.html

Satre, J. (1991) Being and Nothingness. London. Routledge.

Schaffer, H. R., Emerson, P.L. (1964) Patterns of Response to Physical Contact in Early Human Development. Journal of Clinical Psychology and Psychiatry. 5 1-13

Schiller, F. (1992) Paul Broca: Explorer of the Brain. Oxford University Press. London. In Lewis, T., Amini, F. Lannon, R. (2001) A General Theory of Love. New York. Vintage Books.

Siegler, R., DeLoache, J. Eisenberg, N. (2011) How Children Develop. New York. Worth Publishers.

Simpson, J. S., Collins, W. A,, Tran, S. S., Haydon, K. C. (2007) Attachment and the Experience and Expression of Emotions in Romantic Relationships: A Developmental Perspective. Journal of Personality and Social Psychology. 92 355-367

Skyner, R. A. C., Cleese, J. (1993) Families and How to Survive Them. New Delhi. Cedar Books.

Steele, C. M. (1988) The Psychology of Self-affirmation: Sustaining the Integrity of the Self. In Berkowitz L. (Ed) Advances in Experimental Social Psychology. 21. New York. Academic Press.

Sullivan R. (2002) Labyrinth of Desire: Women, Passion and Romantic Obsession. Oxford. Perseus.

Takahashi, K (1986) Examining the Strange-Situation Procedure with Japanese Mothers and 12 Month Old Infants. Developmental Psychology. 22 265-270
Tallis, F. (2004) Love Sick. London. Random House.

Talmon, Y. (1964) Mate selection in Collective Settlements. American Sociological Review 29 491-508. In Tennov, D. (1999) Love and Limerence; The experience of Being in Love. New York. Scarborough House.

Taylor, M. (1999) Imaginary Companions and the Children who Create Them. New York. Oxford University Press.

Taylor, M., Carlson, S. M., Maring, B. L., Gerow, L., Charley, C. M. (2004) The Characteristics and Fantasy in School-age Children: Imaginary Companions, Impersonation and Social Understanding. Developmental Psychology. 40 1173-1187

Taylor, M., Mannering, A. M. (2007) Of Hobbes and Harvey: The Imaginary Companions Created by Children and Adults. In Goncu, A., Gaskins, S. (Eds) Play and

Development: Evolutionary, Sociocultural and Functional Perspectives. New Jersey. Erlbaum.

Teck, K. L. K. (2011) Obsession in Love and Games: Through the Study of Limerence. Inter-Disciplinary.net.

Tennov, D. (1979/1999) Love and Limerence; The Experience of Being in Love. New York. Scarborough House.

Tennov, D. (2005) A Scientist Looks at Love and Calls it Limerence: the Collected Works of Dorothy Tennov. GRAMPS. Retrieved on 7th October 2012 http://www.gramps.org/limerence/

Thich Nhat Hanh (2009) You Are Here: Discovering the Magic of the Present Moment. Massachusetts. Shambala Publications.

Tolle, E (2001) The Power of Now. London. Penguin Books.

Uvnas-Moberg, K., Francis. W. R. (2003) The Oxytocin Factor: Tapping the Hormone of Calm, Love and Healing. Cambridge. Da Capo Press.

Wakin, A., Vo, D. B. (2008) Love-Variant: The Wakin-Vo I.D.R. Model of Limerence. Inter-Disciplinary – Net. 2nd Global Conference; Challenging Intimate Boundaries. Retrieved October 5th, 2012, from http://www.persons.org.uk/ptb/persons/pil/pil2/wakinvo%20paper.pdf

Webber, C. (2012) How to Mend a Broken Heart. USA. Bloomsbury.

Westbrook, D., Kennerley, H., Kirk, J. (2011) An Introduction to Cognitive Behavioural Therapy: Skills and Applications. London. Sage.

Wilson, D. (1999) Perfect Smile by Semisonic. On album Feeling Strangely Fine. Philippines. MCA.

Wittstein, I. S. (2007) The Broken Heart Syndrome. Cleveland Clinic Journal of Medicine. 74 1

Wick, J. Y., Zanni, G. R. (2008) Hypochondria: The Worried Well. Consultant Pharmacist. 23 3 192-194

Willmott, L. A., Bentley,. E. (in press) Exploring the Lived-Experience of Limerence: A Journey Towards Authenticity. The Qualitative Report.

Zhao, X., Nan, X. (2010) Influence of Self-affirmation on Responses to Gain vs Loss-framed Anti-smoking Messages. Human Communication Research. 36 4 493-511

Zukav, G., Francis L. (2002) The Heart of the Soul: Emotional Awareness. London. Simon & Schuster.

Bibliography

Aron, E. N. (1997) The Highly Sensitive Person. New York. Broadway Books.

Brach, T (2004) Radical Acceptance: Embracing Your Life with the Heart of a Buddha. New York. Bantam Books.

Brach, T (2010) Awakening the Love that Heals Fear and Shame. London. Rider.

Byron, K. (2006) I Need Your Love - Is That True? How to Stop Seeking Love, Approval, and Appreciation and Start Finding Them Instead. New York. Three River Press.

Cushnir, R (2009) The One Thing Holding You Back: Unleashing the Power of Emotional Connection. New York. Harper Collins.

Dowrick, S. (2002) Intimacy & Solitude. New York. Norton & Co.

Fisher, H. (2011) Why Him? Why Her?: Finding Real Love By Understanding Your Personality Type. New York. Henry Holt & Co.

Hall, E. (2012) Lust, Love and Limerence, a Short Story. E-book.

Kirshenbaum, M. (2005) Everything Happens for a Reason: Finding the True Meaning of Events in our Lives. New York. Three Rivers Press.

Kornfield, J (2009) The Wise Heart: A Guide to the Universal Teachings of Buddhist Psychology. New York. Bantom Books.

Morin, J. (1996) The Erotic Mind. New York. Harper Perennial.

Perel, E. (2007) Mating In Captivity. London. Hodder & Stoughton.

Reynolds, S. E. (1983) Limerence: a New Word and Concept. Psychotherapy, Theory, Research & Practice. 20, 107-111

Scott Peck, M. (1990) The Road Less Travelled. Arrow New Age. London.

Thich Nhat Hanh (2006) True Love: A Practice for Awakening the Heart. Massachusetts. Shambala Publications.

Thich Nhat Hanh (2010) Together We Are One. California. Parallax Press.

Tolle, E. (2009) A New Earth: Awakening to Your Life's Purpose. London. Penguin Books.

Yongey Mingyur Rinpoche (2010) Joyful Wisdom. London. Bantam Books.

Recommended Reading List

Baumeister, R. F. Wotman, S. R. (1992) Breaking Hearts: Two Sides of Unrequited Love. New York. The Guilford Press.

Bradshaw, J. (1990) Homecoming: Reclaiming Your Inner Child. Bantom Books. New York.

Fisher, H. E. (2004) Why We Love; The Nature and Chemistry of Romantic Love. New York. St Martin's Griffin.

Heaversedge, J., Halliwell, E. (2012) The Mindful Manifesto. New York. Hay House Inc.

Tennov, D. (1999) Love and Limerence; The Experience of Being in Love. New York. Scarborough House.

Tennov, D. (2005) A Scientist Looks at Love and Calls it Limerence: the Collected Works of Dorothy Tennov. GRAMPS. http://www.gramps.org/limerence/

Tolle, E (2001) The Power of Now. London. Penguin Books.

Virtual Support Resources

For caring, sharing, and support, there are online communities such as Limerence.net (http://limerence.net/), as well as *Limerence Experienced (http://tribes.tribe.net/limerence)* and *Experienced Project*, (http://www.experienceproject.com/groups/Have-Limerence/40992).

There are also many related online support communities regarding unrequited love, which include limerence, such as *Unrequited Love (http://health.groups.yahoo.com/group/unrequitedlove/)*.

There are limerence specific online self-help guides, such as (Love and Limerence http://www.love-limerence.com/) and About Limerence (http://bthaw.blogspot.co.uk/)

Limerence related blogs can be found at Psychology Today (http://www.psychologytoday.com/blog/here-there-and-everywhere/201209/limerence-in-love-obsessed-or-both/comments) and with the Addiction Expert David Sack (https://twitter.com/DrDavidSack)

Note. URL's correct at time of publication.

Research

There is currently very little research or information available to Limerent Experiencers or for those who would like to support them such as therapists and medics. If you would like the opportunity to be invited to take part in our research projects, please send your email contact to us at studycommunities@gmail.com

For confidentiality purposes, please note our contact email to you will say: *"Hi, we would like to invite you to take part in a research study. If you would like to be sent an invitation, then please respond to this email. Best wishes. Lynn & Evie"*.

Follow us on facebook

https://www.facebook.com/pages/Love-and-Limerence-Harness-the-Limbicbrain/428882367203296

Authors

Dr Lynn Willmott is a University Associate Lecturer who has a CertHE, degree, Master's and PhD related to Health, Social Psychology, Education, and Applied Health Psychology respectively. Teaching and Consultancy includes Child Development and Health, with interests in attachment, bonding and therapeutic writing. She is a Fellow of the Higher Education Academy.

Evie Bentley is a Psychologist, a successful writer, psychotherapist, and clinical hypnotherapist. Her therapeutic practice is based in West Sussex, England. Evie trained in Oxford at the National College of Hypnosis and Psychotherapy. She holds a master's degree from St Hilda's College, University of Oxford.

Printed in Great Britain
by Amazon